CREATIVE WALL-HANGINGS & PANELS

CREATIVE WALL-HANGINGS & PANELS

Audrey Babington

Arco Publishing, Inc.

New York

*Photographs not otherwise attributed show the work of the author
and were taken by Richard Carpenter*

Published by Arco Publishing, Inc.
215 Park Avenue South, New York, N.Y. 10003

© Audrey Babington 1982

Filmset in Monophoto Century Schoolbook
by Latimer Trend & Company Ltd, Plymouth.

Library of Congress Cataloging in Publication Data

Babington, Audrey.
  Creative wall-hangings and panels.

  Includes index.
  1. Wall hangings.   I. Title.
TT850.2.B33   746.3   82–1834
ISBN 0–668–05603–7   AACR2

Printed in Great Britain

Contents

Introduction

Walls have been decorated with fabric hangings for centuries—the very large ones had the advantage of providing warmth and decoration at the same time. The famous Bayeux tapestry is not, in fact, a tapestry at all, but a stitched wall-hanging, made to record an historical event. Although the colours have faded slightly, considering its enormous length it is in a remarkable state of preservation—a fact which should give encouragement to anyone embarking on a less ambitious wall-hanging today.

At the other end of the scale were the small samplers, sometimes using a great variety of stitches, recording family events, biblical quotations, or the alphabet, in minute cross-stitches. These samplers were often put under glass, in a frame, so some of them have survived very well.

The most noticeable feature of nearly all these wall-hangings is the consistency of the materials and the technique. Today we are fortunate in having a huge range of threads and fabrics at our disposal, giving enormous scope for creativity and originality. Experiment can be taken further by the use of collage—adding interesting odd-ments such as curtain rings, shells, beads and so on. Also we are mixing embroidery techniques in one piece of work—thus quilting, free-stitchery and gold work may be used to interpret one design. Fabric dyes, paints, crayons, inks and felt pens have opened up new vistas in the use of colour.

Another important change which has come in recent times is in the designs themselves. In the past, they were seldom created by the embroiderer. They were either worked from a handed-down pattern, purchased from a designer or worked from a transfer. But people of all ages are now discovering the excitement of creating their own designs—it is not always an easy thing to do, but it gives great satisfaction and a sense of achievement.

Wall-hangings are regarded as an art form, and many well-known artists are using them as a

Wall-hanging made by Rita Fisk for a City & Guilds course, using a wide variety of techniques, stitches, threads and fabrics. The buildings were worked separately, then joined together (Jeremy Marshall)

'Through My Window', a panel in appliqué with simple stitchery. Marquetry wood is used for the fence and roof edges and under the windows. By Dorothy Walsh

means of expressing their talents. Older people with a limited knowledge of either art or stitchery are discovering a new talent in themselves, creating wall-hangings of individuality, colour and beauty. Students and children, working separately or collectively, are experimenting widely with materials and methods. Fabric, thread and stitchery now have an established place in art and crafts teaching at all levels.

To add an additional dimension to this book, a number of well-known professional embroiderers, many of them also teachers, have written a short account of their personal approach to their work. They illustrate deeply-felt thoughts and ideals which they endeavour to express in their embroideries. They show clearly how the attitude to embroidery has changed and point to new directions for the future.

*

Personal Approach—Moyra McNeill

Town and Country

Fabric and thread have always intrigued me, even as a child, as they can so readily be constructed into different shapes by sewing, knitting or crochet, or one can be superimposed on the other to bring about a change in texture or colour. Then there is the paintbox allure of a group of coloured threads, but unlike paint each thread has its own intrinsic texture, whether shiny, matt, lustrous, hairy, twisted or smooth. These observations lead naturally into experiment with the decorative qualities of embroidery techniques, which despite the modern connotation of 'fabric manipulation' are all versions of thread and fabric manipulation. Art school impressed the necessity of seeking 'good shapes' before developing design in colour and texture and opened a view of the limitless permutations of fabric and thread. In recent years trees, or rather groups of trees, have been a recurrent source of design, particularly the mass-space-mass horizontal divisions of ground, tree trunks at spaced intervals, supporting the solid canopy of lush summer leaves, familiar in parks and woodlands of urban areas. Another constant of urban living are crowded roadways; the continuous procession of cars of all sizes and shapes, plus a cynical view of the near-adoration of them by their owners, have led to a series of embroideries based on car themes, often in silver thread to emphasise their transitory brittleness.

My belief is that embroidery can be used as a medium to express ideas or as effective decoration of dress or household items, and that either is a valid expression of the craft. (See 'Shady Glade', page 135.)

*

The Longleat Tree, a wall-hanging in the grand manner, commissioned by the Sixth Marquess of Bath to mark Longleat's 400th anniversary. Embroidered by Amanda Richardson, the centre panel has a rich mixture of fabrics applied to a moss-green velvet background; the dark blue velvet panels were worked by the Royal School of Needlework in traditional style, the leaves and roses being in long-and-short stitch over felt shapes. The stems are raised by using satin stitch over string. A successful combination of modern and traditional methods (Longleat Press Office)

9

TYPES OF HANGING

Stitched wall-hangings can be divided into three main categories:

1 Soft or loose hangings, with no rigid mounting board or frame, though sometimes with a rod for hanging and with weighting at top or bottom. They may be composed of one or several layers of fabric, and are frequently finished with a fringe or similar decoration at the lower edge. Ecclesiastical designs are often made up this way.

2 Panels, mounted on a rigid board or outer framework, without glass. They give the greatest scope for originality in design and mounting, as their shape and size can be whatever you choose.

3 Glazed panels, mounted on a rigid board, covered with glass and usually mounted in a rigid outer frame. The use of glass limits the size and shape of the panel but gives the work excellent protection.

MAKING-UP

Having designed and stitched a wall-hanging, making-up is essential to complete the work and

can add immeasurably to its final effect. It is usually tackled by the person who made the hanging, as last-minute changes can be more easily made, especially with loose hangings and unglazed panels.

Making-up work is often postponed (sometimes indefinitely!) once the design has been worked and enthusiasm wanes. But it is always worth completing work on which much time has been spent, and mounting can be achieved at a very small cost. Finishing generally has been a neglected aspect until recently—embroidery has been presented in an unimaginative, stereotyped fashion with little regard to the individual possibilities. Today a much more personal approach is appreciated.

The best way to make up your work will of course depend on which of the three types of hanging you have made and on the kind of stitchery or techniques used. For instance, a fabric collage without any protruding pieces incorporated could be made into a glazed panel. If the collage has beads, etc, or other raised texture, then it would be suitable for a panel. It would be unsuitable as a soft hanging, as the edges of the fabrics would probably not be finished off all that securely. Ideally the mounting to be used will have been decided upon in the early stages of the design.

Chapter 9 goes into detail about the various methods of making-up, many of them inexpensive. Many different combinations can be used, and the subject is open to experiment—which I hope will be encouraged by the examples and directions given in this book. Study the descriptions of the basic procedures, then tackle the job with confidence and firmness: the latter is meant to be taken literally, for it is surprising how much strength is needed to cut hardboard and pull fabrics taut. Remember always to leave enough fabric round the edge of your embroidery work to allow easy mounting; it can be trimmed off at the appropriate time, and it is comforting to realise that even when a fabric has been glued to a mounting board, any of the sides can be pulled free and reglued if necessary to remove any slight wrinkling.

All the procedures described here are basic guidelines, so experiment according to inclination. The methods here work well, but if you find ways that suit you better, use them.

'Greenhouse', a large soft hanging on natural linen, with handpainted background. The fabrics used include organdie and cellophane for the greenhouse. Machined with black and white cottons, using straight and zig-zag stitches. Hung on a wooden rod. By Irene Hill

Personal Approach—Jan Beany

Surface Preoccupation

Although I was trained as a painter and lithographer, I now prefer to work with fabrics and threads. However, my early training has definitely influenced me. The subject matter has changed but my preoccupation with surfaces continues. Texture and colours over-printed are the main characteristics of lithography, and I have always been fascinated by contrasting paint qualities, such as areas built up in paint applied with a palette knife and the patient build-up of glazes. I found that fabrics, threads and the many varied surface qualities of embroidery techniques could expand scope for creating interesting surfaces for my panels and hangings. The tactile and pliable qualities of cloth offer a vast range of textured finishes which can be opaque, silky, ridged, hairy or of a loose open weave. These can be layered, patched, cut away, padded and manipulated into dozens of arrangements. Added interest of disciplined or haphazard threadwork can develop the work further.

I have tried to explain my strong feelings for textile surfaces but the difficulty is always to discipline myself not to let these factors become more important than the main composition I wish to create. For many years, aspects of landscape have provided me with a wealth of ideas. In the main I like to capture a fleeting moment in time, a peculiar light which in a few brief seconds can completely alter the tones and colour of a particular place, highlighting a certain feature which is usually not so obvious, creating an intimate atmosphere, a magic moment that is rarely seen. Although some may interpret this as a romantic approach, it is nevertheless based on a sincere gut feeling which haunts me until I try and interpret my feeling in a piece of work.

My reference can be anything from odd jottings and notes on the backs of envelopes to quite detailed studies in colour. Latterly, to emphasise a particular feature, I have taken sections out of context or chosen to leave out parts of a view so that the space which is left highlights a certain point. Once I have decided on my approach, I make a simple drawing to the required size,

carefully retaining the main shapes and spaces. These lines are then transferred to the ground fabric. After this planned stage, the remaining areas are then built up intuitively with fabrics and stitchery, trying to keep the balance between the image I have in my mind and the fact that threads and fabrics tend to take a course of their own.

One decision that must be made early is whether the work is going to hang or be stretched over a board or stretchers. If a flowing, undulating soft work is wanted, stretching will spoil the soft textile surface. If the spaces left unworked are very necessary to pinpoint other shapes, then a stretched panel might be best. Another aspect when designing is to find ways of showing colour and tone changes as the viewer walks from one side of the picture to the other. This particularly interested me when I was striving to show the changing light on cliff-faces.

I never aim for a photographic or literal interpretation, believing in exploiting an artist's licence when necessary. I am most concerned in creating an atmosphere, an overall feeling where tones, colour and shape never seem to stay the same. Everything is always changing.

MAKING WALL-HANGINGS IN SCHOOLS AND COLLEGES

Children and students of all ages enjoy the challenge of making a wall-hanging, either for their own personal satisfaction, or as part of a group activity. Projects with fabric and thread do not appeal to all, but for many they are an enjoyable means of self-expression right through adulthood.

Boys as well as girls enjoy exploring the variety of textures, colours, shapes and patterns created by hand and machine methods—swing-needle machines have a special attraction! Even quite young children enjoy the patterns made by hand stitches, and though they may appear to find them difficult to master at first, they show great triumph when it suddenly 'comes right'. As soon as the basic procedure is understood, en-

'Thrift Cliff' by Jan Beany. Hand and machine appliqué—silks and rayons applied to calico. Wool and cotton threads are worked in straight stitches, knots and eyelets (Roger Cuthbert)

couragement to experiment can be given—there are no inhibiting influences, and some original work usually results.

Fabric collage is a good starting-off point for all ages, as good visual impact is quickly obtained, with little of the tediousness sometimes associated with other types of work. It is a valuable means of learning about shapes, colours and textures, which often leads naturally to a desire to learn about other forms of embroidery.

Schools and colleges in fact have many advantages when working with textiles. The wide variety of art and craft activities they practise can be a stimulating source of designs: personal paintings and drawings, cut-paper work, lino and fabric printing; scraper-board work, graphic work, photography, and so on are all to hand. So are useful materials—drawing paper, pencils, paint, wax crayons, charcoal, adhesives, stapling-gun, etc. Advice and encouragement can be given by a variety of qualified staff, and there is plenty of wall space to display work.

Materials for wall-hangings need not be expensive. Children or students can usually obtain background fabrics from home, or from jumble sales, etc. Some threads will need to be bought, but as they will be shared out large spools are justified. Everyone will contribute to collecting other threads, beads, collage items, etc, from various sources mentioned in the book, and a surprising variety results.

Mounting should be kept fairly basic, though old picture frames can be refurbished if available.

The woodwork department might be pursuaded to make some simple wooden frames (unmitred) from lengths of wood, on to which fabric could be stapled. Group projects can be made up in a number of ways:

1 A long 'Bayeux'-type hanging can be made to fit a certain area. Using calico or curtain-lining material as a background, try depicting local or national events. The main outlines can be transferred to the fabric by one of the methods explained later in this book, and interpreted with fabric collage, stitchery, fabric paints, etc, using a limited colour scheme for a unifying effect. Mount it on hardboard with a stapling gun, or hang it on a dowel rod.

2 Each person can work a small design on a given theme, eg birds, fish, the town, etc, to be mounted on the same-sized shape, a small rectangle for instance. They could then all be joined together with cord, rings, bamboo or dowel, etc (see 'Mosaic', Project 15, page 169).

3 A patchwork hanging, using the same shapes or several different ones, can be effective. The colours should be limited, though all the different tones of one colour could be used. This type of hanging would benefit from a lining.

4 Several people can work on a banner-like hanging; bold shapes, appliqué and machine stitching, would be suitable.

5 Individual efforts relating to the same theme are sometimes placed together to form one unit. When the display is finished, it is easily taken down and returned to its owners.

1 Materials and Tools

FABRICS

For making wall-hangings you may need three categories of fabric.

1 Large background pieces on which the design is worked. A wide range of fabrics are suitable, from cottons, linens and fine woollen materials to heavier velvets, furnishing fabrics and canvas. Hessians are very popular, but inclined to fade. Generally, large backgrounds intended for surface stitchery should not have too dominant a pattern or texture, as that would detract from the decoration you are going to add.

2 Smaller pieces of fabric for applying to the background, if you wish to make a collage. As many types as possible should be acquired as a store, to be used when wanted—cottons, woollen fabrics of all weights and textures, corduroys, satins, nets, chiffons, lace, furnishing remnants. They need not all be purchased from a shop—cast-off clothing and jumble sales are a cheap source of supply, and friends are usually helpful in passing on unwanted scraps.

Leathers, suedes and felts, gold and silver kid, etc, should be stored separately.

3 Backing fabrics—thin cotton sheeting, curtain lining, etc are used mainly in quilting and padding, or are placed behind a thin background fabric to give added strength.

Unusual backgrounds

A number of unconventional materials and fabrics could be used for wall-hangings, and give scope for experimental work.

Scrims: there are several different sorts—window-cleaners' scrim, which has a fine mesh, and plasterers' and builders' scrim which has a coarser, open mesh. They fray easily, so allow wide margins when working with them. They are obtainable in shades of fawn and brown, and are very reasonably priced. They are ideal for expe-

'*Three Seasons*': three panels are worked and mounted separately, then joined with twisted insertion stitch, the whole being mounted on paper-backed hessian. The colourings add interest to the simple design—the top section is in various greens, the middle section glows with golden tones and the bottom is rich with orange and browns. A narrow band of appropriate batik fabric has been incorporated, with various stitches, threads and braids.

15

rimental pulled work, needleweaving, free-weaving incorporating collage items, and woollen embroidery. They dye well, and because of their open texture look effective mounted over a coloured background.

A range of linen scrims are also available— they are rewarding to work on, but rather expensive.

Paper-backed felt and hessian: felt and hessian can be obtained bonded to a paper backing—this gives them a smooth, semi-rigid quality, which is ideal for hangings, both as a background and for cutting into shapes.

Plastic-coated materials: a number of different plastic-coated fabrics are available, used mainly in lampshade making. They are stiff enough to work on without a frame, and will hold collage and 'found' items well.

Fine cane window-blinds: these, in natural pale fawn, can be bought in different sizes, at reasonable prices (often less than the price of a frame). The spaces between the canes allow the needle to pass through easily, and thin or thick threads can be used. The pale cane could be painted or sprayed with colour, before stitching, and a variety of items—fabrics, beads and 'found' items—can be incorporated.

The window-blind cord should be removed, and then the hanging is ready finished, without the need of any other mount or frame; being rigid enough on its own.

Rush matting: small squares of rush matting can be used individually or joined together as required. Larger mats, of different sizes and shapes, are also reasonably cheap. Again, bold treatments should be used; simple felt shapes, for instance, would look effective, incorporating other materials as required.

Interlinings

These are used to stiffen and give 'body' to a hanging or fabric. They may be quite thin, or thick and fairly rigid. An interlining should be chosen to suit the hanging, and the purpose for which it is required. Materials generally used are tailor's canvas, cotton duck, thick calico, sailcloth, deck-chair canvas, buckram, Vilene or blanket.

Vilene have developed a wide range of interlinings, for use on all types of fabrics. Some are stitched into place, others are ironed on, bonding to the fabric.

Transparent iron-on: for transparent fabrics, eg chiffon, voiles, etc, enabling easy handling of these sometimes difficult materials.

Bondaweb: this acts as an adhesive, and can be used on lightweight and mediumweight fabrics. Fabrics can be applied to each other, when ironed together.

Superdrape: this is the only iron-on interlining recommended for large areas. It is particularly useful on soft hangings, allowing the material to hang naturally.

Heavyweight Vilene (sew-in): it can be used for soft hangings and some appliqué methods.

Temporary fabric support

When thin fabrics need to be machined on a single layer only, it is advisable to back them with a temporary support. Several different materials can be used, according to suitability:

Paper: tissue, greaseproof or wall-lining paper. Pin and tack it into place, stitch through it as required, then tear it away.

Vanishing muslin: use it as paper. It is ideal for very fine fabrics and is unusual in that, being a combustible chemical gauze, it can be ironed away. The heat of the iron dissolves it—the residue can be brushed off. This ironing-away can be done through a protective layer of paper, but if there is any risk to the fabric simply tear the muslin away.

THREADS

The wide variety of commercially produced threads gives a near-infinite variety of colour and texture. Stranded embroidery cottons are available in many colours. *Coton á broder* is a thin, twisted thread. Pearl thread is made in different thicknesses, with an attractive sheen and colours. Soft embroidery is a thicker, matt thread. A number of thick threads are often sold wound on spools, and are specially useful for hangings requiring bold stitchery: Stalite, Lyscordet, Crysette, for example.

Crochet thread can be bought in many different types—thin, matt thread, lustrous rayon thread, in unusual colours; and some thicker threads with Lurex, in gold, silver and bronze, which have richness and sparkle.

There are some interesting macramé threads—tubular rayon, and strings in a variety of thicknesses and textures.

Other miscellaneous threads are found in hard-

ware, gardening and fishing shops—raffia, twine, cord, etc.

Woollen threads are produced in an enormous variety of colours, textures and thicknesses. Knitting wools range from 2-ply, which is very thin, to chunky wools like rug wool. Crewel wools sold for canvas work, and darning wools are useful, being sold in small quantities. Other wools are bouclé, mohair, angora, Lurex, chenille and a number which vary in thickness along their length. Wools made for weaving, or by weavers, provide subtle colours and a range of textures.

Unravelled knitted garments are a useful source of supply. Wind the unravelled wool round a book, tie it into hanks, then remove it from the book. Wash it gently in warm soapy water, and put it to dry; rewind loosely when dry.

Gold and silver threads are available in different weights, and are an asset when interpreting a design which needs richness. They are usually couched, and although they are expensive if used exclusively, they are effective used in a restrained manner in certain areas of your hanging.

'The Dustmen'. A wide variety of fabrics are used to emphasise the heavy nature of the job shown. The scaling of the figures gives depth and distance; note the simple treatment suggesting the wall. By Angela Schmid (Colour Centre Ltd, London)

MISCELLANEOUS TOUCHES

Braids, ribbons: all sorts of braids, ribbons, laces and so on can be incorporated into wall-hangings, and can be obtained from haberdashery departments, craft shops or discarded clothing. Other items from various sources should be collected—bandage, gift-wrapping cords, tape, and so on, which can be couched, machine-stitched or threaded.

Beads and sequins: these are invaluable to add extra interest and texture. They are available in small packets from craft shops, and larger beads, especially wooden, are sold for macramé. Sometimes necklaces can be bought quite cheaply, especially from market stalls and charity shops. Ask for broken necklaces, too—these are often available.

Sequins can be bought in a range of colours and shapes, in packets or by length.

Rings: collect as many different types and sizes as possible—small washers, picture-hanging rings, curtain rings (metal and plastic), eyelets, rings from jewellery, bangles, etc. Materials may be metal, plastic, wood, bone, and so on. Large wooden rings for hanging curtains are often used as a decorative feature—this could be copied for wall-hangings.

Rings can be used as a basis for design in a number of ways—grouping them, or forming different patterns. They can be covered with thread (buttonholed) and used with other materials, eg beads, bamboo. (See 'Green Rondels', page 79 and 'Spring Green', page 120.)

Wire: all types of wire might be used, bare or plastic-coated. Very thin, soft wire could be used for couching, lacing or threading. Small beads can be threaded on to wire and formed into shapes. Wire can be covered with thread, either by hand or machine, formed into shapes, and the spaces filled with needle-weaving, buttonhole filling, machined openwork, etc (see Project 16, page 170).

Wire can also be used to make a cut shape firm, by stitching the fabric edges over it on the wrong side.

Chain: metal chain can be obtained in many types—very fine, used for necklaces, to bath-plug chain or large, heavy links used outdoors for fencing, etc. Jewellery, haberdashery, hardware and gardening departments should be explored.

Metal mesh: there are many different types of wire mesh—some have fine holes and are quite rigid, others have much larger holes and are more pliable. The fine mesh can be cut to any shape, and is sufficiently rigid to hold a variety of collage items. It is advisable to cover the edges with masking tape while working. Bold stitchery could be used—the technique for making pin and thread designs looks very effective.

Coarser mesh could have the holes altered by enlarging the spaces. Raffine, string, raffia, cords, tubular rayon, etc, would cover the mesh quickly.

Plastic tubing: this is usually reasonably priced, is available in different widths, and can be clear or coloured. It could be couched, formed into shapes, threaded with cords, etc; cut into different lengths; or made into 'beads' by cutting into small pieces—these can be buttonholed with thread before use, if required.

Steel mesh, calico and thread combined to give a fascinating three-dimensional texture. By Jane Hubbard

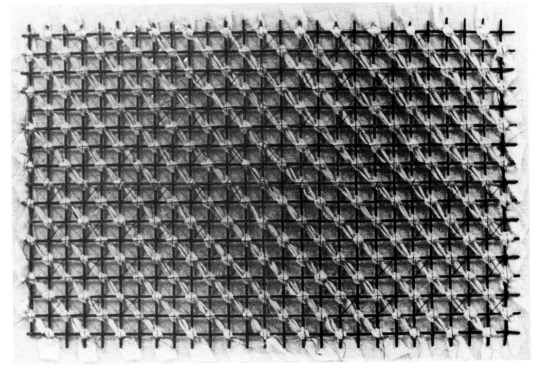

It can also be used as an unusual mount for scrims, etc. Shape it into the required 'frame', then stretch the fabric over it and stitch into place. Useful in particular to make an oval or other curved shape.

Plastic netting and mesh: plastic garden netting has a distinctive texture which could be used in small pieces; or use it as a background fabric for experimental work.

A surprising variety of plastic mesh is found in greengrocers' and gardening departments, containing vegetables, fruit and nuts, bulbs, etc: fine and coarser, green, orange, red, yellow, etc. The mesh can be stretched tightly to open it out; cut into shapes; applied over other fabrics; cut into strips for threading or couching; bunched and stitched to give texture, etc.

'Found' objects: innumerable objects can be collected from a huge variety of sources; look particularly for items with a hole in them, or that will allow the needle to go through them. Try out small pieces from broken machinery—cogs, nuts, spindles, etc. Metal weights for fishing have different shapes, and many have a hole through them. Beech mast, acorns, small pebbles, shells, bones (soak in a weak solution of bleach), feathers, unusual buttons and a host of other items are suitable for inclusion on hangings. (See 'Sea Shells' Project 3, page 150.)

TOOLS

Needles: a varied assortment will be needed.

Beading needles, which are very fine, for small beads.

Sharps for general-purpose sewing.

Embroidery needles, with long eyes, for stranded cottons, etc.

Darners are longer, with a long eye, for woollen threads.

Tapestry needles, with blunt points, are generally used on canvas.

Chenille and carpet needles, and bodkins, are extra thick and strong with large eyes for tapes and other thick threads.

Curved needles are useful to stitch awkward areas, eg when stitching one fabric-mounted board to another, and may also be helpful to handicapped people. Kidney needles, with a blunt point, would be useful for canvas work. They can be obtained from surgical suppliers, in packets of two, at modest cost.

Upholstery needles can also be obtained curved.

Pins: dressmaker's steel pins, and also some plastic-headed pins.

Scissors: a pair of sharp dressmaker's scissors for cutting fabrics; small embroidery scissors with sharp points; a pair of scissors for cutting paper.

Embroidery frames: there are several different types of frames which will hold the fabric taut while it is being worked.

The ring or tambour frame consists of two wooden hoops which fit inside each other. They are obtainable in several different sizes, and are useful for not very large designs, or for placing over certain areas.

A *rectangular slate frame* requires more preparation, but is specially useful for canvas and gold-work, as the background is less likely to pull out of shape once mounted in it. There are several varieties.

An *old picture frame* makes a quick temporary frame—the fabric is held in place with drawing-pins, or stapled to it. This is a very useful method, as the fabric can be removed very quickly.

Artist's stretchers are made from lengths of wood slotted together; these can be used to make a frame of whatever size is required. The fabric is then drawing-pinned or stapled to it.

A *simple wooden frame* can be made from lengths of wood (unmitred) fixed together with wood glue and panel pins. If a stapling-gun is available, staple the fabric neatly to the back of the frame, pulling it taut. This works well for small or medium panels.

Using a frame for some work is a matter of personal preference—some people find them restricting and others don't feel happy without one. A great deal of embroidery can be worked successfully without a frame, especially larger pieces, but care should be taken not to pull the stitching tightly, or the work may pucker. Do not bunch up the fabric in the hand—keep it flat, on a table, stitching evenly. Make use of the non-stitching hand to keep the work flat and even.

A frame is essential, however, for machine embroidery and helpful for hand quilting, needle-weaving and appliqué, gold work and black work.

Sewing machine: a sewing machine can be a useful aid in making wall-hangings, but is not essential. It will be used in varying degrees, according to personal inclination and the methods employed. Some wall-hangings are entirely machine-stitched, using appliqué, machine embroidery, collage, patchwork or quilting tech-

Table-top frame, particularly useful for canvas work though also can be used with thick background fabrics. Lightweight and collapsible (Readicut Wool Co Ltd)

niques. An ordinary straight stitch machine can be used successfully on some simple designs, for patchwork and quilting, but a swing-needle machine is essential for free machine embroidery; and the zig-zag stitch is useful for attaching fabrics to a background, couching threads and braids, etc. The stitch can also be used—with discretion—as a definite pattern element. Closed zig-zag stitch forms satin stitch, which looks very effective when worked with a machine embroidery silk, which has an attractive sheen.

Adhesives: there are many different adhesives now available, to suit a wide variety of purposes. They are becoming increasingly useful as an aid for all forms of creative textile work, but care should be taken that the correct one is used. Some of the glues have special qualities which can be exploited in creating designs, so experiments should be made.

A selection is listed below.

UHU is a colourless, all-purpose adhesive, which will stick almost anything except polystyrene and polythene. It is sold in tubes with a narrow nozzle—this is useful to ensure a sparing application and for directing it to a precise spot. It is quick-drying.

Copydex is a latex glue, sold in tubes and jars. It is useful for mounting fabrics on card and board. If re-positioning is necessary, the fabric can be pulled away and re-glued.

Evostik is made in different qualities, so choose the correct one for the material—for paper, wood, etc.

PVA adhesive, eg Marvin Medium is versatile and particularly suitable for porous materials—paper, fabrics, string, etc. It can be used neat, or diluted with water. Fabrics can be stitched without difficulty when they have been stuck with it.

Araldite; Bostik 7; Epoxy resin (plastic-type) are two-part glues, the contents of two tubes being mixed together to form a permanent bond. Use with polystyrene.

Spray-on adhesives are used for photographic work, and are expensive, but spray application is an advantage for flimsy materials such as organdie, chiffon, nets.

Polycell is a cellulose powder, used mainly as a wallpaper paste. It can be used for paper, card and fabrics.

STORAGE

A system soon becomes necessary! Try storing fabrics in large plastic bags—group them into colours, but keep special pieces, velvets, nets, etc, separate. Larger lengths of fabrics are better kept in a chest of drawers, old trunk or suitcase. If creases may be a problem, use a strong cardboard roll, or piece of polythene drainpipe.

Large plastic sweet-jars are often obtainable from sweet shops—braids, wools, ribbons, string, etc, could be stored in them. Glass jars, of different sizes, with screw-topped lids will hold beads, assorted rings, etc, which can be easily identified.

Various types of storage boxes can be found in hardware, craft or hobby stores—those made for small screws, fishing tackle, and so on, are invaluable for sequins and small beads.

Wooden or plastic cutlery trays are useful for threads, cottons, etc, especially for work in progress.

2 Designing

A single figure, 'The Punk', deceptively simple in outline, conveys chilling realism. The design originated from a photograph. The figure was built up from four layers of felt, graduated in size, emphasising the different areas of the body, covered with black gloving leather stab-stitched into place. The background and pavement are worked in shades of grey, with silk thread, and the milk bottles in straight stitches of white silk. Finished work is mounted on hardboard (covered with flannelette sheet), then placed on a larger board covered with dark grey moygashel and stitched into place with a curved needle. A metal frame finishes the picture. By Julia Tulip (Embroiderers' Guild)

Designs for wall-hangings can be achieved in many different ways, and people who feel they are not good at drawing can take heart, because countless methods can be used to produce a design. The eye and the mind can be trained to perceive and select design elements by constant practice. Cultivate the habit of looking in a positive manner, and it soon becomes second nature to do so.

Museums, art galleries, exhibitions, should be visited—they are much more imaginatively arranged nowadays, and contain a fascinating variety of colours, shapes, textures and patterns. Keep a look-out for a good basic shape which offers scope for imaginative treatment. Birds, flowers, leaves, fish, shells, butterflies, and so on, are obvious starting points. Zoos, stately homes, gardens (other peoples' or your own), could also provide a variety of ideas for designs.

Annual exhibitions of craft work are held all over the country, and contain work of a high standard. Weaving, stained glass or jewellery designs can spark off an idea, or suggest an unusual colour scheme. Wall-hangings are frequently featured—study methods used to interpret designs and making-up.

When considering a design for a wall-hanging, shapes, lines, texture and colour are involved. Generally, the shapes are the most important element in the early stages—the other aspects are decided gradually, plus the technique. It is surprising how many things have a simple basic outline—a fish, feather, leaf or church tower, for instance. Look at the chosen shape carefully for lines within it which give it character. Preconceived ideas are not always reliable—for example, the vein in a feather does not often run straight or centrally. Looking and observing is never wasted, and the design will benefit when it comes to adding the details.

A sketch book should be used to make a record (whether expertly drawn or not) of observations and ideas. This too will become a pleasurable habit, and results will show an increasing appreciation of form, line and pattern.

Whichever method and source you select from the following suggestions, to create a design, it need only be regarded as a starting-off point and need not be adhered to slavishly. Approached in this way, an original design evolves. It is important to carry out various experiments in producing designs in a variety of ways. This will develop a deeper appreciation of design, and even if many of the results are never used, the knowledge gained can be used to advantage eventually.

COLOUR AND TONE
Fabric and threads, dyes, paints, crayons and pens, combine to give an incredible range of colours, which form an exciting element in the making of wall-hangings. Because the choice is so vast, careful selection is essential for a successful result. The colours used in one piece of work should usually be limited or it may look confused and lack unity.

Some knowledge of colour theory is an asset, but use of colour is more or less instinctive; it can be developed by constant experiments in varied media, some of which are suggested in this book. By becoming more aware of everyday things and surroundings, our appreciation of the wide range of colour and its variations will be heightened.

Colours can be warm or cool, and are affected by one another. A dull, uninteresting colour will often look surprisingly different when placed next to, or on top of, another colour.

A colour scheme based on related colours may be very pleasant, but look a little dull: an accent of an unexpected colour, used in small amounts and imaginatively placed, will add liveliness and impact. In colour schemes where large amounts of bright colour are required, do not use equal amounts—one should predominate, balanced by the others. A neutral colour can be used to separate them, which will have a calming effect.

The tones of colour used should be varied, so that there are shades of light and dark to give interest to the design. Care should also be taken that the proportion is varied—equal amounts of colours of exactly the same tone will not give a satisfactory result. It is challenging to work a design in different tones of one colour. Variety is

'The Lane' in straight stitches, using a mixture of knitting and crewel wools. The fabric was worked on a frame to get an even tension. The small light spaces in the trees play an important part in the naturalistic effect. By Eirian Short (Denys Short)

achieved by placing threads, stitches and fabrics in different ways, exploiting density, space and light.

SPACE
This can play an important part in a design—as an area around it, or as an integral part of it. If it is used for the former, enough of the background fabric should be left unworked to give the effect of a 'frame', which will add emphasis to a design. Spaces can be included as an essential part of a design, providing a 'quiet' area for the eye, allowing for a better visual appreciation of the other parts.

FOCAL POINT
Most designs are more satisfactory if they have some focal point to lead the eye first to one important part of the design.

SOURCES OF DESIGNS
Collect pictures: make a collection of interesting pictures, which could give ideas for shapes,

colours and textures. Keep them in a folder or scrapbook, and separate them later into subjects—birds, gardens, buildings, and so on. Obtain them from magazines, newspapers, greetings cards, calendars, wrapping papers, wallpapers, etc.

Photographs: if you like photography, this could provide another source of design ideas— sometimes in the most unlikely places! It is particularly useful in recording something of interest, when time is short.

Posters: some very attractive posters are available which could easily be used as the basis of a design, especially as they are often the correct size for a wall-hanging. The subject should give scope for imaginative use of fabric and thread. For example, there are some beautiful posters of birds of prey, which would be fascinating to work in a variety of threads and textures to suggest the nature of the bird.

Tracings can be taken of the outlines of the subject, which could be used as a pattern for fabrics and thread.

The outline of the 'Osprey' was lightly marked on window-cleaner's scrim with felt pen, then freely stitched, using stem-stitch filling, and interlocked fly stitches on the wings, mainly with woollen threads. Mounted on pale-coloured hardboard in a plain wooden frame

Maps: try using a map of your own area as a basis for a design. Ordnance Survey maps give clear outlines, which could then be developed, filling in areas made by the road patterns. Historical maps are often more pictorial, and suggest treatments for the different shapes of fields and so on.

Natural form: here is a vast source of designs, so it is advisable to focus on a few aspects which have particular appeal, and use them as a basis. Leaves, flowers, shells, fish and insects, feathers, for instance, could be interpreted in countless ways: see the 'Feather' in Project 4, page 151, for one example.

Simple sketching, however basic, will be helpful to clarify shapes and patterns. A special study, gathering material from a number of

24

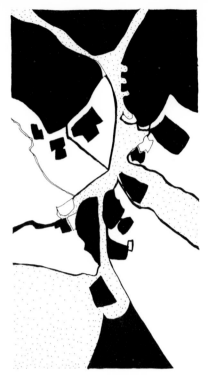

Using a map as a design source

Monstera leaves with their irregular-shaped holes can be grouped to make a design for cutwork, pulled work or appliqué

Leaves are so varied that they can be fitted to any design

Spiky sea holly makes intriguing shapes

Petal shapes can be emphasised with narrow bands divided by a space (known as 'voiding')

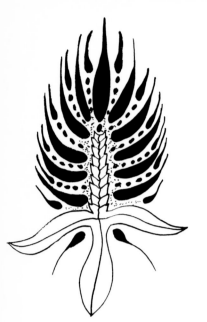

The decorative qualities of plants can be developed in countless ways. With a teasel, try emphasising the form

Design taken from an old tile

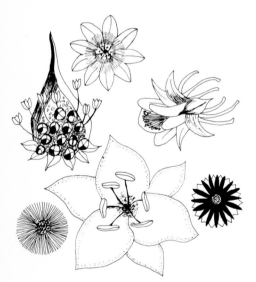

Flower heads

The flowing movements of fish can be captured with couched threads, stitchery and machine embroidery

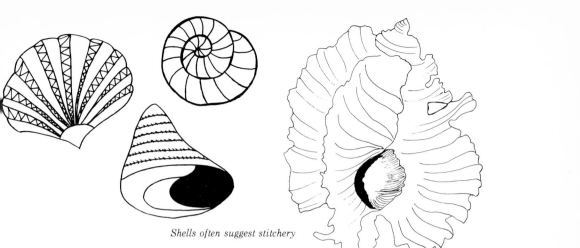

Shells often suggest stitchery

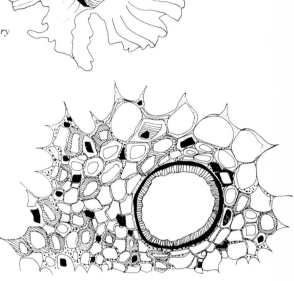

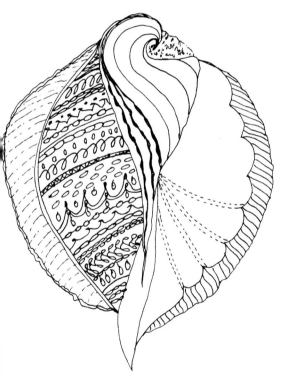

(above and below) *Biological specimens put under the microscope, whether seen in photographs or actuality, can suggest interesting ideas for embroidery*

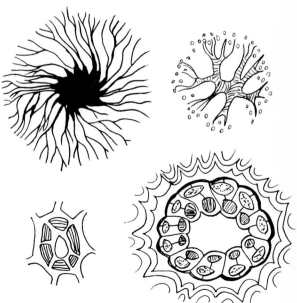

This design originated from an X-ray photograph of a shell; it was used on an oval-shaped panel, with white fabrics and threads on a grey shot-silk background. The left side was worked separately on cream flannel, in different varieties of chain stitch, with many different threads, narrow braids and some beads. It was applied, with some padding to raise it above the rest of the design. The right side was made from white satin, with corded quilting. The centre was formed with a textured cream crepe in shallow folds, slipstitched into place

Animals may have simple outer shapes that can be used for interesting pattern work

Paint or dye on an old toothbrush can be used to make sky or water patterns. Practise on spare fabric to acquire skill in achieving different densities

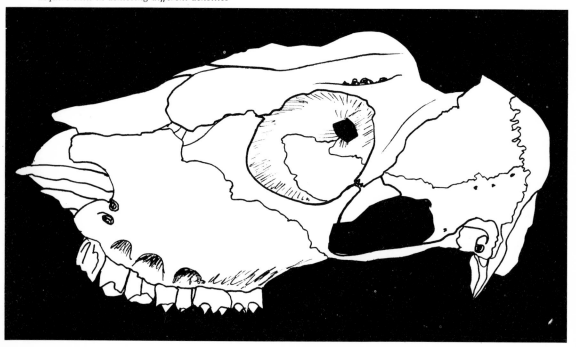

The lines and crevices of an animal skull could be used to develop a design

different sources, eg personal observation, nature books, magazines, and so on, is a rewarding approach.

Magnified cellular structures suggest unusual colours and patterns—if no microscope is available, biology text books and magazines could be studied. They would make very good starting-off points to be developed with fabric and thread, scrims, etc, using techniques such as pulled thread, quilting, machine embroidery and needleweaving.

Many different types of design can be made using the human form—a figure alone, a group, or just a head-and-shoulders shape. There is an amazing variety of approaches from which to choose from the most basic simplicity—using a rectangle or triangle, for example—to elaborate decorative presentations. Attempts at realism are often not very successful; it is usually more rewarding to find a design element which can be emphasised with the technique used. Ideas can be found in museums and art galleries, in your own photographs and pictures, sketches, books, magazines and so on. (See 'Dustmen', page 17, 'The Punk', page 22 and Project 11 'The Family', page 160.)

Appliqué, collage or canvas work could be used to work designs, which could also be interpreted with a strong linear quality, using metal thread for example. Facial features can be omitted, if it suits the design—this can be very effective. Facial colour can be added easily with fabric paint or crayon, giving just the amount of skin tone required.

Birds are a rich source of design, as there is so much scope for interpretation of shapes, colours, textures and patterns. Designs can be based on a single bird, a group of birds, on birds as part of their surroundings, or on a real or imaginary exotic bird.

We have a wealth of sources for such designs—personal observation and photographs and sketches, books and magazines; wrapping papers and greetings cards; museums and zoos, and so on. Many of these sources provide a ready-made shape, often to the correct size, which can be traced off and used as required.

Fabric paints are particularly useful for bird designs, both for the background, which need not be given any further treatment, and for the bird or birds themselves, which can be painted and then have stitchery added. The other fabric-

Formed from simple fabric shapes, the children playing have a lively, expressive quality. By Helen Clarke

From a brass rubbing

Sketch of part of a modern stained-glass window in a church. The faces are repeated several times in bright clear colours

29

An unusual design with interesting possibilities, from an advertisement. The vertical lines are filled in, creating shapes with a slightly irregular look. Graph paper could be used and designs evolved for blackwork, canvas work, etc. Personal family scenes could be created, and the bold house shape used as the outer shape of the panel (Federated Employers Press)

Traced from a bird book, then enlarged for a glazed collage panel; the pigeon was made predominantly white with touches of pink and blue. A bright blue background fabric made a pleasing contrast with the bird and the white frame

A humming-bird used in an advertisement might have been drawn with embroidery in mind—French knots, blanket stitch and fly stitch (Bovis Ltd)

'Birds' by Kate Downhill. Negative and positive shapes give impact to a basically simple design which could be interpreted in appliqué, blackwork or quilting

Groups of birds have interesting shapes

Trees have special significance for many people. Embroidery can express their shapes, forms and colours and their relationship with the landscape. Make sketches, collect photographs, etc, to build up a personal reference source

printing methods suggested in this book can also be tried. (See the batik panel illustrated on page 56.)

Suitable techniques are quilting and padding; collage and appliqué; canvas work; metal thread; and even rug-hooking.

Stitches used for interpretation could be stem stitch—placed close together and used for outlining; fly stitch, particularly when the stitches are fitted together, one inside the other, graduating in size; and single Roumanian stitch, taken from the bird's head to the tip of its beak, then caught down in the centre with a tiny stitch.

Trees are a great inspiration, singly or in groups, set in landscapes or used on their own; try to observe them wherever possible, their shapes and density and colours, and their relationship with their setting.

To use landscapes on your wall panels is not nearly as difficult as beginners often think. A sketch of the main outlines is all that is needed. It is more interesting to create a design that has some personal connection for you, a piece of country nearby perhaps, or one where you had a holiday. Designs can also be developed from colour photographs, your own or something in a magazine or book. Trace or draw the outlines on

to a sheet of paper, working to the size required for the finished embroidery. This can then be used as a pattern.

Alternatively, shapes for fields, hills, etc can be cut out freehand and used to build up the design, with careful choice of varied fabrics and textures.

Man-made objects and surroundings: this is a wide field being far more often explored today. It offers a wealth of exciting shapes and forms. Machinery, tools, factory equipment, coal mines, building sites, scaffolding, provide strong images which would translate well into a design for a wall-hanging, and would be particularly relevant in a town or city setting.

Buildings, too, have well-defined outlines, but vary so much in character that a wide range of interpretations are possible. Note the different patterns made by the roof formations, brickwork, windows and doors. Shaped mounts could be planned for the finished work, and if feeling ambitious, several buildings could be worked separately and then joined together, to make an unusual long panel.

Designs could be worked out with cut paper shapes, or drawn on to a piece of paper the required size for the finished work, then a tracing taken from it.

32

*The stark shapes of factory buildings contrast with the
irregular billows of smoke from their chimneys*

'*Cathedral Close*' (Exeter City Council)

Large country houses often have features that lend themselves to embroidery. In this drawing the formal lines of house and garden contrast with the rough foreground. By Diana Smith (Director, Dillington House, Ilminster)

Taken from an early drawing of the west front of St Paul's Cathedral—a ready-made design for canvas work

(above and below) *Buildings seen in silhouette make a dramatic impact which can be interpreted in appliqué, quilting, fabric collage and so on. Magazine photographs can be traced and enlarged as required*

Personal Approach—Sheila Page

Environmental Element

I find it difficult to categorise my work, though I do feel drawn to strong, bright colours, simple shapes, and frequent use of figures. Each piece is a personal response to a poetical element, often found in the mundane—shops and market stalls; city parks and back gardens; a newspaper photograph, and so on.

Having trained at the Glasgow School of Art, then lived in the heart of Cardiff, a recent move to a rural part of Scotland has given me a dramatic change of environment, which will, I feel, influence my work in the future. I am already becoming absorbed with gentle and subtle colour schemes, the shapes of clouds and trees, and the gentle pace of country life.

I enjoy using a variety of fabrics, though silk is my favourite. I deliberately keep stitches simple, to put across the message contained in each piece, in the most direct way. (See 'High Fliers', page 136.)

*

DESIGNING FOR SPECIFIC SITUATIONS

It is satisfying to design a hanging for a particular room or situation. The colours, style and position of other furnishings should be taken into account. Different rooms give scope for quite different types of hangings; you can provide a focal point in bedroom, hall, dining-room or study, or give interest to a dull area.

Decisions should be made on the position, size and type of hanging you want: soft or a panel? Glazed or unglazed? In a small room, a long narrow panel, using colours in the furnishings, could be arresting, and even in a large room, a small hanging placed in a recess or near the door could be effective.

A large hanging gives scope for bold treatments of shapes, colours and textures. On the other hand, if there are already a number of dominant features a hanging in quiet colours could be more what the room needs. If there is a special motif in curtains, carpets, etc, this could be used as a basis for designs, enlarged if necessary and developed.

When placing a hanging in position, remember not to put it too high if it has intricate detail.

'Sampler' by Joan Sutton. The design is based on husband's and wife's christian names, worked on canvas of 14 threads to the inch and backed with denim. A great number of canvas stitches were employed, with a wide variety of threads and added materials including padded silver kid, sequin waste, beads, etc. In shades of blue and green—from deep navy to pale green. The silvery sparkle of kid and sequin waste provide eye-catching relief through the overall richness. The panel hangs from a chrome rail with macramé loops and hanging cord. The fringing follows the shape of the design formed by the letters.

35

Lady Banner for Coventry Cathedral, by Margaret Nicholson. Worked on a natural slub fabric in gold thread, gold kid, crystal beads, pearls and shisha glass, the design conveys richness and an almost sculptural quality; several techniques are used. The reverse of the banner shows a Crown of Thorns, the design based on the grille of the Chapel of Christ at Gethsemane. The two sides of the banner are fastened together with press-studs so that they can be detached (Uming Wright-Watson Associates Ltd)

Naturally, the size of the hanging and the height of the room will have to be taken into account.

It is also rewarding to design a hanging for a particular person, based on hobbies or interests.

A Church Hanging

The vast interior of a church poses special problems, which should be taken into account, when planning a design. Bold, simple shapes will make an impact, if the hanging has to be viewed from a distance. Although fussy detail should be eliminated, the embroidery should also provide interest at closer quarters, so textures and fabrics should be carefully chosen. The proportions of the hanging should suit the position—scale is of particular importance. Many churches have small inner chapels, which create a private, peaceful atmosphere: for these, hangings can be of a more detailed nature, giving the eye and mind fuller satisfaction.

The colours of the brickwork, windows and furnishings are another important consideration. Fabrics and threads should be finally selected in the building—colours vary according to the light that falls on them. The exciting range of fabrics available today has contributed to the freer approach to ecclesiastical designs. Furnishing fabrics are particularly suitable—used with appliqué, patchwork, goldwork and machine embroidery, designs can be bold, colourful and vigorous.

Fabric paints and dyes have also considerably increased the scope for lively work. Sewing machines can be used to speed up some or all of the work, according to the nature of the effect required.

Careful planning of the design is essential, and it is advisable to draw it full size on a piece of paper the actual size and shape of the intended hanging. It is rewarding to design for a particular season, when colour and subject have a special significance. Every effort should be made to reflect present-day trends, and not copy accepted 'safe' symbols.

A communally produced hanging can be a very satisfying project, if carefully planned. It is usually more successful if one person is in charge, overall, with everyone having a clear idea of what they are to do. It is important that a confident and encouraging atmosphere is created—mediocre work results if a timid approach is adopted.

SAMPLERS

We are all familiar with the samplers which were worked in the past. They usually consisted of very fine stitches, and in Victorian times were made almost entirely in minute cross-stitch. With the renewed interest in stitchery, many people are again finding pleasure in making a sampler, using a wonderful variety of threads, colours, stitches and fabrics. A number of suggestions are given here for satisfying ways of making samplers, which are more interesting if they have a special theme, or are based on a definite shape. Use:

Straight, wavy or irregular lines: these are quick to do, look attractive and make a useful record for future reference. Have a theme—'Harvest', 'Blue Skies', 'Strata', etc.

Abstract designs: based on squares, circles, etc, these can be worked out with cut paper patterns. (See 'Wall Sampler' Project 18, page 171.)

Simple shapes: these can be broken up, then filled with patterns—eg fish, feather, rhinoceros.

One colour or one stitch (with variations): a challenging method which would be enjoyed by anyone with a working knowledge of stitches and threads.

One technique: eg blackwork, metal thread, canvas work or pulled fabric.

Mixed techniques: put two or more together as you like.

Baptistry panels for Salisbury Cathedral, designed by Audrey Chorley. The centre panel is octagon-shaped, a symbol of baptism. Sea-coloured furnishing fabric slubbed with mauve and green represents Living Water and is machine-embroidered to indicate underwater currents. The central fish, in silver kid and fabric, is padded with felt and embroidered with metal threads and beads. The lettering is in dark blue, and the twelve fish, representing the Apostles, in gold and silver. At the top of the panel the Agnus Dei is worked on canvas, stretched over a fret of wood. The wools used match the pinkish-grey of the cathedral walls and the stitches emphasise the characteristics of the lamb—petit point, French knots, rice, diamond cross, cut and uncut velvet stitch. The banner is made from red and white leather, wired to hold the shape of the folds.

On the side panels, Alpha and Omega are worked over seven layers of felt with laid metal threads, and gold and silver kid over string. Seven lamps and a dove, representing the Seven Gifts of the Spirit and the Holy Spirit, are worked to match the fishes. The oil in the lamps is shown by silk and gold organza over kid and the flames are in pleated gold fabric. The chains— handmade from purls in chain stitch—proved to be most challenging: the slightest deviation in line on any of the four chains on each lamp caused the tension to be lost, and the oil appeared to spill out, extinguishing the flames! This was remedied by stitching against the edge of a long ruler.

The centre panel was laced over hardboard and applied to a shaped insulating board covered in stone-coloured fabric. The lamb is held slightly away from the panel with a small block of wood. The side panels are stretched over softwood frames, tacked to them and lined with a damp-proofed fabric. (Melvyn Fatherly, by permission of the Dean)

37

Small shapes: use these to fill an area—leaves, fish, birds, for instance.

CIRCULAR WALL-HANGINGS

These are usually made up as an unglazed panel, as circular frames fitted with glass are difficult to obtain, and a loose hanging would not hold the shape. Designs can be evolved from a number of sources—flower heads, jewellery, wood knots, the sun, for example. They need not have a *central* focal point—off-centre is sometimes more intriguing.

Designs can also be made by using a circular cut-out 'window' on a larger design (see 'Isolating a design' drawings . . .) or by cutting drawing paper to the size required (use compasses or

plates, etc) and planning the design on it (see 'Reptiles').

Circular panels can be mounted on board, wooden bases for basketry, hoops, cake-boards, metal lampshade rings, etc. Larger designs could make use of discarded dartboards, bicycle-wheel rims, metal hoops from barrels, etc.

It is sometimes easier to work a circular design if it is mounted first on the foundation. This works well with net, scrims, needle-weaving and pulled work.

Circular embroideries

38

be tedious to put right, and the fabrics may be spoilt. Hand stitching is slower, but allows better manipulation of the fabrics and gives a softer finish to the work. Machine stitching gives a stiffer appearance, which can be used to advantage for some wall-hangings. If machining one fabric on another, some puckering may result (especially on circular pieces) if inadequate preparation is made—tack fabrics into position first. This will also ensure the fabrics do not move out of place.

Experiments on a small scale will help to assess the merits of each type of stitching—for example, a landscape of fields in different fabrics could all be machine stitched on the background; but a more satisfactory result may be achieved by machining field patterns separately on some of the fabrics, then hand stitching them into place on the background.

An interpretation of a wood-knot rubbing, using various different stitches (drawn by Camilla Nock)

MACHINE STITCH—OR HAND STITCH?

Stitching by machine or by hand each has its own merits and suitability. Machining is very quick, but sometimes this can be a disadvantage—if a mistake is made in haste, the unpicked work can

'Sun'. Golden fabrics and threads give a dazzling effect. Gold lamé fabric, padded and applied in sections, is finished with braid and tassels. Bamboo is held in place with blanket stitch. The centre has a bold backstitched wheel edged with braid and ribbon, and the middle section is filled with weaving. It is mounted on a piece of lightweight ceiling board—easy to cut with a sharp knife.

'Reptiles': mainly surface stitchery, with applied net
on the cobra. Chain-stitch filling is used on the newt on
the right, with knotted buttonhole filling on the central
newt and fly stitch on the snakes. Padding was added
to the outer reptiles after the embroidery was completed
by adding a thin fabric backing, stitching with a
matching thread; this cotton backing was slit, stuffed
with kapok, then stitched up again with a few
overcasting stitches. The dark green outer fabric mount
has a texture chosen to suit the subject.

3 Ways of Creating Designs

Paper collage: this is made by creating a design with torn or cut paper shapes, using different textures and colours. The design can be based on natural form, on man-made objects or be abstract in concept. A concentrated period of observation should be allowed first. Then the papers should be cut or torn into shapes quickly, and stuck down. Tissue paper, coloured magazine photographs, wallpapers, wrapping papers, sweet papers, etc, could be used.

Mixed collage: a wide variety of items could be collected—pulses of all shapes and sizes, seeds from flowers and plants, macaroni and rice, string, cords, etc. The design should be carried out on stiff card, and a quick-drying adhesive used—UHU or Marvin Medium, for instance.

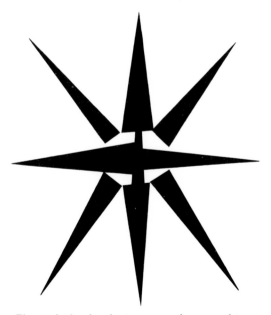

Elongated triangles of cut paper can be arranged to make an arresting design—suitable for an ecclesiastical hanging (drawn by Camilla Nock)

Designs made in glued collage can be freely interpreted with fabric, thread, beads, etc, using a variety of techniques such as stitched collage, canvas work, padding, gold-work, etc.

Cut paper designs: creating designs with cut paper shapes is quick and effective. It is also versatile in the number of ways it can be used. Use different papers and thin card, cutting them into a variety of shapes—haphazardly or premeditatedly—squares, oblongs, crescents, leaf shapes and so on. Stick them on to a contrasting piece of paper. It is a good idea to cut the shapes to the size required for the finished work—they will then be ready for use.

The actual cut paper pieces can be used in a number of ways:

As templates for cutting out the fabrics.

To draw round, or use as a guide for a tacking line, on the background fabric.

As a base for fabrics—tack fabrics on to the card shapes with extra fabric for turnings, then stitch them into position on the background. The card can be left in.

The cut paper design can be traced off, and the tracing used to transfer the design to the background with tailor's carbon (see page 60).

Folded paper designs: paper can be folded in various ways, using paper measured out to the required size of the design, or making smaller patterns to develop within a shape. Pencil lines can indicate a special shape, or shapes can be cut freehand, experimentally. Leave the central fold intact, but if mistakes occur, see if they can be made into a design by sticking them on to a background paper.

Complicated patterns could be used to make couched-thread designs; simpler shapes could be used for appliqué, quilting, etc.

A simple cut-paper shape can be drawn around and placed in varying positions. When the outline is filled in an interesting design may emerge

Folded paper can be cut into simple or intricate designs; try using negative and positive shapes together, as in the long narrow design

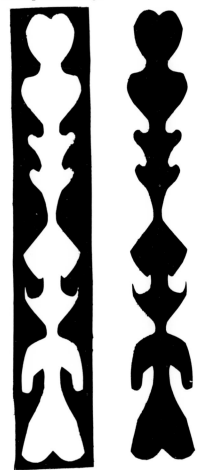

Isolating a design: the placing of a cut-out 'window' shape over a larger picture, photograph or drawing, etc, gives emphasis to certain areas, suggesting an original design. Make a 'window' shape a rectangle, circle, oval, etc using stiff paper or card. Alternatively, use two angles of card—and fit together. Move the card about over the picture, looking for an interesting composition of shapes and patterns. If the cut-out shape is the size required for the design, it can be traced off and used without alteration.

Breaking up basic shapes: designs are often made with good basic shapes, and although they may be quite simple they can be divided up to give different areas of interest. Lines of tacking can indicate the sections—they should be varied in size and shape, to avoid a dull effect (see 'Rhinoceros', Project 13).

Some areas are usually easier to work than others, though often some parts can be left plain to offset the others. Some stitchery can be worked closely, some spaced out, to vary the tone and textures. Very often, while stitching one section ideas for the others will be suggested, as threads, beads, fabrics, are selected and sorted. Drawings can also be cut up and rearranged, so try some experiments. Colour magazine pictures could give you some unusual and subtle designs.

Lettering: interesting designs can be made using letters—a Christian name, the alphabet, etc. Cut out letters in paper or card, and arrange them on a piece of paper, the required size of the

Using a cut-out 'window'

43

The 'window' can be any shape

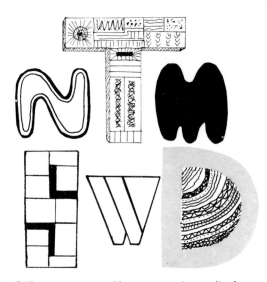

Different treatments of letters, suggesting appliqué, stitchery, patchwork

Newsprint can suggest patterns. So can letters, perhaps turned back-to-front and jumbled

finished work. The letters could be distorted slightly, or made to fill a space, touching each other. The letters can be cut in fabrics, or filled in with threads and braids, etc. Alternatively the letters can be left plain, and the spaces around them embroidered.

One initial letter could be embroidered, then mounted on a board or card, cut in the shape of the letter—it could be made any size, and would make an impact if worked boldly and hung on a plain wall.

Designs with letters are particularly well-suited to appliqué, quilting, and machine embroidery, though they can be worked successfully in most techniques.

Wax-crayon rubbings: practically anything with a raised surface can be experimentally rubbed with a wax crayon. Place a piece of thin white paper over the surface, and rub evenly over it with the flat surface (not the point) of a wax crayon. Coins, leaves, bark and wood-knots are obvious examples. Manhole covers, plaques, etc will give larger rubbings.

Thin card shapes could also be rubbed. Stick them on to a background, then rub them, moving the paper around to vary the design, if required. Subjects could be buildings, a shoal of fish, flying birds, flames, people, etc.

A collage of scrap materials could be assembled—small washers, pieces of embossed wall-paper, string, cocktail sticks—to give a variety of patterns to rub.

PVA medium can be used, by 'drawing' a pattern on a stiff base of card, using the nozzle to produce a thin raised line. The quick-flowing adhesive will give a spontaneous design, which can be rubbed when dry.

Church brasses are usually rubbed with a

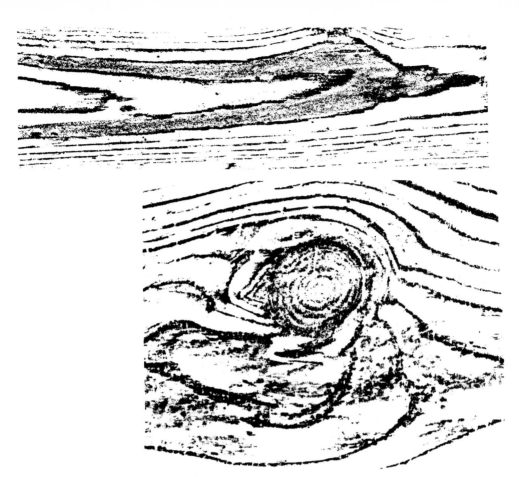

*Wax rubbings from wood; the knot has been used in
several different ways as shown in this book*

*Marvin Medium was squeezed on the smooth side of
corrugated card and rubbed when dry; the corrugated
lines have also come through with pressure from the
rubbing*

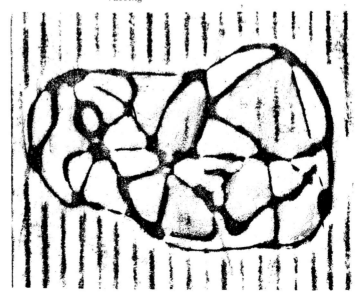

Brass rubbings—dispense with background details not required (Devon Brass Rubbing Centre)

methods of procedure and materials. If the designs are required only as a basis for a wall-hanging, these centres are a convenient way of obtaining them.

Wax crayons can also be used to create quick, effective designs, using 'etching' techniques.

Painting a shadow: select a suitable subject, then hold it steady in a strong light over a piece of paper; paint the actual shadow, in black paint. Such designs can be used for appliqué, collage, stitchery or quilting, and for painting on fabric.

Quick free-painted designs: If paint and brush are used freely, you can get an interesting basis for an embroidery.

FABRIC PRINTING

There are a number of ways of printing directly on to fabric now that good-quality dyes, paints, pens and crayons are available. They have increased the scope for producing original and exciting designs. Some suggestions are given here, but endless combinations are possible; experiment as time allows. Some very quick and simple methods give a stimulating basis for stitchery.

Fabricrayons: Fabricrayons should be used on synthetic fabrics—nylon, terylene, tricel, trevira and synthetic lining materials. The

special wax called heel-ball, and permission should be obtained before commencing. Most brasses require time and patience to rub properly, but they are well worth the effort, a rich source of pattern and designs particularly suited to blackwork and gold-work. Brass-rubbing centres provide a ready source of reproductions for rubbing, and also advise on the correct

Painted shadow

46

Free brushwork with Indian ink or paint can result in unusual designs suited to textural work. This rough sketch is based on a newspaper photograph of a burning building

A large design can be drawn on paper with Fabricrayons, then ironed off on to fabric: here the paper is being peeled away to show the design

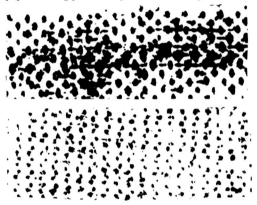

Wax crayon rubbed on to canvas for textural effect

design is drawn on paper first—avoiding papers with a glossy surface. Slightly rough cartridge paper will give a strong colour transfer, as it holds the crayon well. Tracing paper can also be used, a good method if an accurate replica is required. (As the drawing and tracing are laid face-downwards on fabric, the design will of course be reversed.)

The design is positioned carefully on the fabric, then pressed with a fairly hot iron for 20–30 seconds.

Two prints or more can be obtained by re-crayoning the paper design. It can also be ironed off a second time, though it will not be so clear—a fact which could be used to advantage.

Textures can be formed by taking rubbings, which can be cut to the shape required or rubbed direct on to the paper design.

Wax-crayon designs: ordinary wax crayons can be used on a variety of fabrics, to draw a design, take a rubbing and so on. Iron the cloth on the wrong side on to a newspaper to fix the colour. Textured effects can be obtained with canvas, by colouring a design on it, then transferring it to a cloth by ironing the cloth on top of the canvas. Do not let the fabric move while transferring.

Fabric paints: there are several makes of good-quality fabric paints (eg Dylon Colour-fun) which can be used to paint designs directly on to the fabric. It is advisable to practise on scrap material to become accustomed to the right consistency to use, and the best thickness of brush to cover the fabric. The paints are usually used rather dry, giving a different effect from ordinary painting. Water can be added, but this should be done cautiously, as it may run down the grain of the fabric, where it is not required.

The painted design can be used as basis for stitchery, or left as it is, with other areas worked.

Felt pens, etc: permanent-marker felt pens can be used successfully on fabrics, and combine well with other forms of printing and painting. Practise with them first, then use them with confidence for quick and colourful effects.

Splatter printing: this method should be tried out on a small scale, first on paper, with paint or inks. Leaves, ferns, etc, could be used, or a thin card cut-out shape of whatever is required. Place the shape on a white or pale paper, and dip an old toothbrush into paint or ink. It should not be

47

Brightly coloured wax crayons have been used in patches, then covered with black crayon. The design was then scratched through into the layers, making patterns, which could be interpreted with appliqué and couching (Guy Scott)

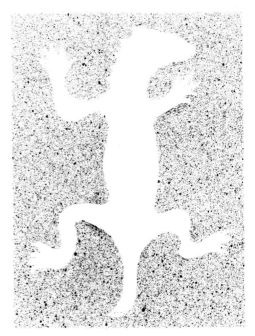

Splatter printing (Camilla Nock)

dripping. Draw an old knife-blade over the bristles, holding it over the paper and guiding the splatter to outline the shape and cover the background. More than one colour could be used. Lift off the shape carefully—it will be plain on the paper, surrounded with splatter effect. More than one shape could be used, or the same shape could be moved on the paper. The splatter could be made in different densities in some areas.

To use the technique on fabric, mount the fabric in a frame (old picture frame, tambour or artist's stretchers) so that it is taut. Pin or tack the chosen shape on to it then splatter with fabric paints or dyes. An effective design could be made by fixing several shapes to fill the space required.

The splattered effect is also useful for backgrounds, surrounding a worked design. Place a mask of paper over the design to protect it while splattering.

Stencilling: a stencil can be cut from oiled manilla paper, acetate, plastic tile—or a piece of card coated with PVA glue on both sides. Using a simple design, cut out the shapes with a craft knife. Pin the fabric on to a board, over a sheet of

Fabric printing can give simple but definite designs; this could make use of graduated colours and be combined with stitchery or quilting

'Sampler'. On a background of rose-pink hessian, this sampler of stitches incorporates a variety of threads, with added fabrics and beads. By Freda Lee (G. Izmidlian)

49

A paper doily was used as a stencil. Charge the brush (perhaps a toothbrush) with paint and draw it firmly over the paper

Experimental printing with a cut-out card shape. An outline tracing of the 'Little Ballerina' sculpture by Degas, made into a silhouette with black ink or paint; it was waxed, then painted with Indian ink to give a mottled effect. Several such shapes used close together would be interesting

smooth newspaper, then fix the stencil into position with small pins. The design can be filled by 'splattering' with an old toothbrush, using fabric dye, or applied with a small piece of sponge. Experiment first, to decide on the best method, and also to check that the dye is neither too thick nor too runny. Lift the stencil away carefully.

A design can be built up using the same stencil in different positions (wipe it clear before re-use). Small stencilled shapes would also be effective if used to fill in parts of a design, eg small birds on a landscape.

'Cotswold Wall'. Irregular fabric shapes, lightly padded, have been wrapped with threads and then applied to the background. Smocking, hooking and French knots add to the texture and combine with the colour to make visual impact with a simple design. By Diana Keay (Valerie Harding)

A whole or part of a paper doily could be used, to make a complete design or form part of one.

Mosaic printing some interesting mosaic designs can be made, using a wooden block the correct size for the design you require. The end of a small wooden stick could be used for small-scale designs—coat with fabric dye, then print all the design in a mosaic pattern, or just the background. The colours can be varied where required. The subject of the design could be worked in another technique, eg appliqué, leaving the mosaic printing untreated.

Canvas-work patterns could also be used as a guide for designs, using graph paper.

Printing with found materials: this type of printing is easier to do if small amounts of fabric paint are placed in the lid of a tin fitted with a piece of moist plastic foam. Press the ends of sticks, cotton reels, corks, etc, into the paint, then print on the fabric. The design can be developed with brush strokes, etc. The end of a square or oblong-shaped stick will print a 'wall' design effectively; string glued on to a wooden block is useful for a range of patterns. Map-pins and drawing-pins stuck into a cork produce spot effects. Iron when dry, to fix the colour.

Tint printing: mix a small quantity of different dyes or fabric paints in jars, making the colours fairly weak. Using a piece of plastic foam, print the fabric by dabbing areas of colour over it. It helps to base the colouring on a subject—eg a rock garden, a landscape, harvest—or to base the placing of the colours on a colour photograph. The colours run and merge into each other. When

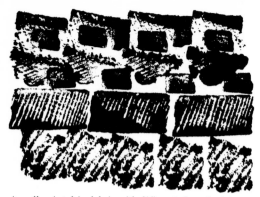

A wall printed in fabric with different-shaped stick-ends, then quilted, with stitchery and French knots, etc, added between the bricks

A sketch of a rock garden was used in designing a panel. The different areas of colour were quickly placed, weak dyes being dabbed with a sponge on to cotton lining material. The rocks were hand quilted, and stitchery used for plants

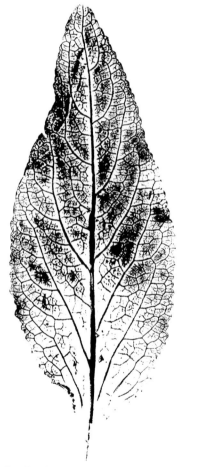

The undersides of leaves often have a pronounced ribbed pattern which prints well on fabric. Leaves could be worked separately and then applied, by hand or machine. Try various fabrics to discover the most satisfactory surfaces

dry, the fabric is an interesting base on which to add stitchery. Iron it first to fix the colours.

*

Personal Approach—Eleri Mills

The Art of Simplicity

Although my work is essentially textile in quality, I am strongly influenced by painting styles, and much of my background work and research takes the form of drawings and watercolours.

The development of any piece of work follows a very involved thought process, and as in any art form, the final statement becomes a vital means of self-expression. Reflections on places, people and atmosphere are translated into visual and textural images.

The subject and the form that a piece of work takes are often elusive and difficult to explain, but the materials I use are generally basic and uncomplicated. Cotton canvas makes a good ground for acrylic paint, applied by brush and sprayed with a mouth diffuser. The threads are usually Appleton's crewel and tapestry wools, and stranded cottons. I stitch entirely by hand, enjoying the simplicity of my materials and tools.

The canvas is pinned vertically for initial painting and spraying, then stitches are worked in, sometimes working on a frame, according to the density of stitching. As each piece is in-

dividual, there is no one repeating work process or pattern. My stitches are based on herring-bone, cretan, feather, and various detached and tufted stitches. I want them to lose all identity as traditional stitches, forming marks which become an integral part of the painted cloth, using the thread in a way that suggests elements of movement, stillness, density or space.

The panel by Eleri Mills commissioned for the library at ICI's Central Toxicology Laboratory, Alderley Edge, England

53

These methods were used for the commissioned panel in the ICI laboratory, which had a long and high main passage within the library area with a vast, imposing wall space which had an almost ecclesiastical quality. The 'feel' and atmosphere of a building should help dictate the form that a commissioned art work should take. I was presented with a dramatic setting for a panel in a quiet library atmosphere, and decided that the piece should combine both qualities.

The subject matter is based on sketches done in the Peak District, forming a design both lyrical and evocative, but with a contrasting strong geometric form with a well-defined upward flow. The scale of the work made it necessary to divide the panel into sections, each worked separately on wooden stretchers.

Cotton canvas was used for the background, with acrylic paint—painted and sprayed. The stitching was worked by hand, in crewel and tapestry wools and stranded cottons. Muslin, organdie, rug canvas and foam were applied to different areas. The heart of the whole piece is in the lower central section, and has bold, energetic stitching with quite brutal colour combinations and textures. This is halted by a strong horizontal blue line, and an expanse of white misty canvas, developing into an ominous sky, with white shapes flying across. The central T shape is hung against a backdrop which is much quieter in mood.

Working with embroidery to produce large-scale panels like this is very rewarding, now that the old traditional barriers have been broken down and a potentially exciting new field in art has been revealed.

*

DYEING

Tie and Dye

Tie-dyeing gives unexpected results, which could be used as a basis for a design. Cold-water dyes (Dylon) with Dylon Cold Fix (or household soda) are the easiest to use. Natural fibre fabrics, eg cotton, are necessary, and if your fabric is new it should be boiled with washing powder to remove any dressing. Old sheets, etc, would be suitable.

Areas on the fabric should be securely bound, to stop the penetration of the dye. Use string,

cord, cotton, raffia, nylon stocking cut into strips, or elastic bands. The binding should be very tight, and fastened off securely so that it doesn't unravel. (Leave some thread hanging, then after binding tie the two ends together.) If several bindings are done close together, use a slip knot to carry the thread to the next position.

Fabric can also be tied into knots—but they can be difficult to undo!

If more than one colour is to be used, dye the tied fabric with the lighter colour first. Dissolve the contents of the tin in one pint ($\frac{1}{2}$ litre) of warm water. Stir well, then pour it into a plastic bowl or a bucket, large enough to submerge the fabric. (Use rubber gloves while handling dyes and fabric.) For each tin of dye, dissolve 4oz (125g) salt and one packet Dylon Cold Fix in one pint hot water. (If you have no Cold Fix, use one heaped tablespoon of household soda.) Stir well, add to the dye, then top up with enough cold water to cover the article. Immerse the article for an hour, stirring occasionally. Take it out, rinse, remove the bindings, and then wash in hot soapy water; rinse again until the water runs clear. The whole process can be repeated, with more bindings and another colour, if required.

NB If there is enough dye, it could be used to dye an assortment of fabrics and threads—simply immerse them all, and leave for a time. They will absorb the dye at different rates, and will have a unity with each other, which could be used to advantage either on the tie-dyed fabric or on a different background.

There are several other different types of dyes, for use on a variety of fabrics. It is important to use the correct dye for each type of fabric, and carefully to follow the directions for whatever dye you obtain.

The random tie-dyed patterns can be developed with stitchery, beads, etc, or used as a background for designs. Plain bold shapes would look effective applied to a tie-dyed background.

Pieces of tie-dye could be cut out and applied to another background. (Bondina could be used to attach it, if necessary.) Or the fabric can be gathered, pleated, ruched, smocked, or used for cut-work or reverse appliqué. It could be cut into strips, rectangles, etc, to combine with other fabrics included in patchwork hangings.

Batik: Wax-resist Dyeing

Batik is an ancient method of creating designs on

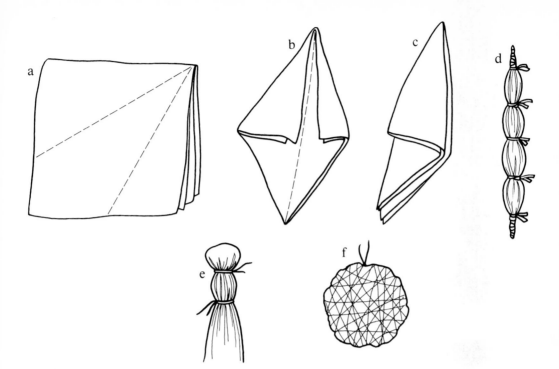

fabric with wax and dyes; the waxed parts of the fabric of course resist the dye. There are two methods—using cold-water dyes and ironing out the wax to remove it, or using Procion dyes and boiling out the wax (which can then be used again). The former method is simpler to do on a small scale. Paraffin wax is used, with some beeswax mixed in if available. White candles can be melted down. Experiments can be made with coloured wax crayons and melted Fabricrayons, which will add extra colours to the design. The design can be drawn on to the cloth with a pencil beforehand, or a random pattern created.

Non-synthetic fabrics must be used, eg cotton, linen, silk. The wax should be heated in a double container over hot water. Small amounts of wax crayons can be melted in small tins, stood in a frying pan of water. As the wax should be hot, extreme care should be taken while dealing with it, and never pour any of it down a sink.

The materials needed are:

Non-synthetic fabric
Wax candles (beeswax if available) or coloured crayons
Pot for melting wax, in a pan of water
Various sizes of ordinary bristle paint-brushes, or printing items

The cloth to be tied and dyed is folded into four (a), then diagonally (b, c) and bound tightly with strong thread or string. Small pebbles can be tied in (e). Or the bundle can be screwed up with crisscrossed thread

Dylon cold-water dyes
Salt
Cold fix (or household soda)
Plastic bucket or bowl
Old picture frame
Drawing pins
Rubber gloves
Absorbent paper

Stretch the fabric over the frame and secure it all round with drawing pins.

Draw the design on the fabric with a pencil, avoiding fussy details.

Melt the wax until hot but not smoking, and brush the design with the wax, placing it where the dye is not required. Alternatively, create a random pattern, by flicking the wax on to the fabric, or brushing it on freehand in a linear pattern. Or you can print the wax on to the fabric, using a variety of objects, eg tops of tins, corks, sticks, pipe-cleaners, card held on edge etc. Hold them with gloves on, or fix them to a stick. Or use a mixture of these methods.

Remove the cloth from the frame. The wax can

'Birds', a batik panel, hand-quilted, with simple stitchery for the trees and leaves. The fabric was dipped into green dye, and when this was dry yellow fabric dye was applied on the birds

Batiks can be given a number of waxings and dyeings, according to the effect required, but for a wall-hanging a fairly simple programme is probably best, and the design can then be developed with stitchery, etc. Even one-colour batiks look effective, and if small amounts of other colours are needed, fabric paints can be used.

Batik designs lend themselves well to quilting and padding, stitchery, collage, machine embroidery and so on.

Polyfilla-resist 'batik': this is an experimental method, which should be tried out on a small scale first. Cover the whole fabric with Polyfilla, and while it is still wet draw the design in it, using a cocktail stick etc. Tin lids and other implements could also be used to make patterns. Leave to dry. Brush dye well into the design. When dry, wash off the Polyfilla.

'Stormy Sky' by Miranda Bertenshaw. The sky has been subtly coloured with dyes, black ink and bleach, on cotton lawn. Stuffed and wadded quilting has been used on the fields

be crackled at this stage, by crumpling the cloth. This results in a fine network of lines of dye, which is an attractive feature of batik.

Dissolve the tin of dye in one pint ($\frac{1}{2}$ litre) of warm water. Stir well, and pour it into the bucket or bowl. Dissolve four tablespoons of salt and one sachet of cold fix (or household soda) in some hot water, stir well, and add it to the dye. Top up with cold water, if necessary, to cover the waxed fabric, which should be immersed for an hour. Rinse it in cold water and let it drip-dry.

If you wish, the fabric can then have more wax added, to retain some of the first colour, and be dyed another colour.

To remove the wax, scrape off some with a spoon or blunt knife. The remaining wax should be ironed out onto newspapers or blotting paper, sandwiching the batik between the layers and changing them frequently. Wash the cloth in mild detergent, dry and iron it. (If there is a wax stain, it can be dry-cleaned.)

Instead of covering the fabric, the Polyfilla can be piped, forming a linear pattern, then left to dry. Brush on dye, crackling the Polyfilla—do this carefully, or it may fall off. Leave to dry, then peel off Polyfilla, wash and rinse.

Flour-resist 'batik': a flour-and-water paste gives a satisfactory resist, and is easier to use than wax, both at home and in schools. The flour should be mixed with water to a thick paste which will pipe—not too runny, nor too thick. Make a few trial pipings, using a plastic detergent bottle with a removable nozzle. Pipe the paste on to the fabric, then leave overnight to dry.

This resist method cannot be immersed in dye. Paint the cloth with fabric dyes, crackling the dried flour, so that the dye spreads into it. Leave to dry, then scrape off the paste. Iron on the wrong side, then wash off any remaining paste.

*

Personal Approach—Jean Davy Winter

Postcard Presentation

My specialised training in printed textiles combines well with embroidery, particularly screen-printing techniques, which allow me to explore the different design aspects in which I am most interested.

My first experiments were mostly concerned with the abstract qualities of the landscape and strong pattern values, such as black and white cows in relationship to the surroundings. Screen printing and embroidery are ideal for translating a series of designs based on a theme.

Recently I became fascinated with the multiple images on picture postcards, and found that they gave me the opportunity to combine a

Jean Davy Winter's 'Pier and Windbreaks'. The strong blue, pink and red of the windbreaks is echoed by the beach huts in softer tones. The screen-printed pier in black and white provides a focal point

number of contrasting techniques in a coherent picture. I used collage, hand and machine embroidery, and quilting, for some beach designs—the simple shapes and brilliant colours of the beach huts and windbreaks made an ideal contrast to the fine black and white detail of the pier, which was screen printed. I mounted them with narrow fabric-covered frames, printed and machined to match the colours in the picture.

Other designs have been based on a collection of old sepia-coloured cards, hand-painted in unnatural colours—vicious blues, pinks and greens. I printed some houses in sepia, used fabric transfer inks to achieve the brilliant transparent colours, and then worked into them with hand and machine embroidery.

There is unlimited scope for developing designs, covering a wide range of subject matter, using a combination of printing and embroidery.

*

DESIGNING WITH THREADS

Designs can be made by taking a textured thread, such as chenille or bouclé wool, and pushing it around on background fabric until an interesting pattern forms. It can be couched down, then filled in with stitchery, fabrics, beads and so on.

A variety of shapes in different materials, eg pieces of thick card, cardboard tubes, pieces of wood, can be covered with fabric, then wrapped round with threads or string and applied to a background (see 'Cotswold Wall', page 50).

Grouping different threads together will sometimes suggest a theme for a design—eg pale, thick apple-green wool, shiny olive-green and bouclé wool could suggest a seed-head.

Stiff threads, strings and cords can be bound together with a thinner thread, using a figure-of-eight movement. They could be used on a large hanging or panel. Cords can also be bound singly, with thin silky threads, wrapped tightly. Different colours can be used on one length, then formed into shapes.

Strings and wools can be coated with a PVA adhesive or Polycell paste, formed into patterns as a basis for designs, then left to dry. The patterns should be made on a board covered with a polythene sheeting (PVA adhesive will not stick to it). Experiment with different types and thicknesses of string, forming patterns by coiling, trailing, etc, or winding it round pins or nails pushed into the board. Leave to dry, then lift off—the string will hold its shape and can be used as required. A whole design could be worked out on the plastic sheet, then placed on the proper background and fixed into position.

String takes dye very well, so it is a good idea to put some into any dye you have available.

Threads can be attached to lampshade rings, thread-bound frames, or eyelets screwed into wooden frames. Needle-weaving, etc, can be worked, incorporating beads and oddments.

DESIGNS WITH STIFFENED FABRICS

Pieces of stiffened fabric can add a different element to a design. There are several methods of stiffening the fabrics of your choice, using various adhesives—try them out first.

Dip loosely-woven fabrics (coarse scrim, for example) in Polycell paste. Place it on a plastic or polythene sheet, push the fabric into holes, folds or what you will, and leave it to dry. Other dipped fabrics can be moulded over shapes (covered with plastic) for 3-D effect.

Dip several thin materials, such as cotton, silk, rayon, lace, nylon, into Polycell paste, then layer them on to a plastic sheet on top of each other, smoothing them and removing any excess paste. Leave them to dry. Draw a design on the top fabric, then cut it out. The layers of fabric will peel away and a design can be made from the different parts. Experiment on a small scale—some fabrics may stick to each other.

Fabric can be bonded to a paper backing with a PVA adhesive. Try paper and fabric on small pieces first. Coat a backing paper with a thin layer of PVA glue. Place fabric on it, smoothing carefully. Iron on the fabric, then turn over and iron the paper with a hot iron, taking care not to scorch. When the stitchery is completed, the paper backing could be pasted to a mount of hardboard.

Bondaweb is an iron-on adhesive and stiffener. If shapes are cut out, eg petals and leaves, then ironed on to Bondaweb, delicate fabrics are just stiffened sufficiently to be formed together to make a three-dimensional shape which will not sag or fray. Flower heads, for example, can be made, and used three-dimensionally in a design.

There are a number of iron-on interlinings which can be used to stiffen fabrics, and also stop them fraying. Practise on small pieces first.

CREATING DEPTH

Depth in a panel gives it an extra dimension, which is intriguing to the viewer and challenging to the worker. It can be achieved in a number of ways, but it should be carefully thought out beforehand, as different methods of mounting are involved. Subjects such as caves, underwater scenes, landscapes, the universe and abstract designs give scope for exploiting depth.

A quickly made wooden frame (unmitred) or old picture frame can be covered with fabric or thread. The top layer could have long threads stitched into the frame, and be needle-woven, buttonholed or wrapped, keeping an open effect. The second fabric or thread layer could be inserted into the back of the frame, then covered with a backing fabric to neaten, perhaps letting the colour of it show through the other work.

Layers of fabric of different weights, nets, scrims, hessians, velvets, leather, felt, can be mounted on varying sizes of window mounts, or stiffened with wire. Cut-work, pulled work and so on could be used.

A variety of objects can be covered with fabric—try lids, pillboxes, stones—and attached to a background. Threads can be strung from them, stitching into the background as required. Beads and oddments could be incorporated.

Mounting can also be done in wooden boxes and drawers, etc, or a specially constructed shadow-box (see Glazed Panels, page 143).

The depth of this box-like panel creates a theatre for 'Clowns', by Belinda Fairclough. It has a backdrop of foil, distorted to provide interesting reflections. The surround has been embroidered on a striped fabric (Terry Waddington)

'Classical Building' by Miranda Bertenshaw. The formal lines of the building are repeated in the shaped 'window' mount, which is held a little distance away, thus creating interesting shadows. The leaves add to the three-dimensional effect; they are made by covering wire with acetate material which is then machine embroidered—and the fabric is then dissolved with acetone, leaving intriguing spaces (Cedric Barker)

4 Transferring the Design to the Fabric

The design can be transferred to the fabric in a number of ways. Take into account the material and method of working, then choose from the following methods:

1 Use a tailor's pencil or washable transfer pencil. Draw directly on to your fabric, round templates, etc.

2 Tack paper or card shapes into position, then tack round them, outlining the shapes. Remove the papers.

3 If the design has inner lines, trace the whole design on to tracing paper. Pin it in position on the fabric, then take running stitches through the tracing paper, along the lines of the design. Carefully pull away the paper.

4 If the fabric is semi-transparent, it is possible to trace the design through it, going over it with a hard pencil very lightly. As pencil cannot be removed, use this method cautiously. Fix the design and fabric firmly, so that it does not move. Alternatively, the lines can be painted, using poster paint and a fine brush.

5 Dressmaker's carbon can be purchased in a number of different colours. It does not smudge. Place it between the fabric and design, and draw over the lines of the design with a sharp pencil. Make sure the carbon, fabric and design are anchored so that they do not move.

6 A special transfer pencil can be used to trace off the design. It is ironed on to the fabric. (In most cases, the design will be reversed.)

7 If an accurate transfer is required, prick and pounce is the best method. Take a tracing of the design, then make small perforations along all the lines, quite close together, using a crewel needle. (Place the tracing paper over a pad of cloth, to keep the holes open.) Place the perforated design on to the fabric, then secure both to a board. Rub a small amount of talcum powder through the holes (add a little charcoal, if the fabric is white). Use an old toothbrush or a small roll of felt.

Remove the tracing very carefully, and join up the dots with a washable transfer pencil; if on velvet or similarly loose-surfaced fabric, use a very fine brush and white poster paint (no water), making a thin line. As your stitching follows the painted line, the dry poster paint should be flicked off.

8 Window method: trace or draw the design on to tracing paper. Pin it to the back of the fabric, or fix to the window with Sellotape. Tape the fabric to the window, then draw over the lines, using a washable transfer pencil or tailor's pencil. If marking delicate fabrics, eg organdie, and a fine marking is required, show the line with a series of tiny dots, using a hard pencil with a sharp point.

ENLARGING OR REDUCING THE DESIGN

The grid method: this is not as complicated as it sounds, and gives accurate results. Place the chosen design on a plain piece of paper, glue it down lightly, then rule a grid of squares over it. Number the squares.

Take a sheet of paper the size required (or rule out the new size on larger paper) and rule the same number of squares on it as are on the first grid. Draw in the design, following carefully the correct positions, so that each part of the design matches up with the corresponding square. Use a dark felt pen, or ink, on the outline so that it can be easily traced.

A projector: to throw the image on to a wall, moving it to obtain the correct size. A paper can be put on the wall, and the projected image (or part of it) traced off. Colour slides can be used, and details enlarged, to make unusual designs.

A pantograph: this is used for enlarging,

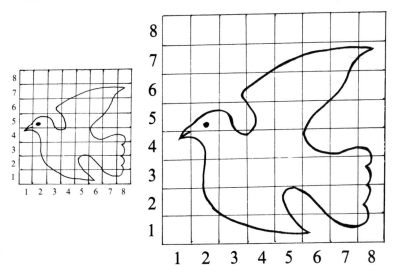

Enlarging on a grid
(sailing ship by courtesy of
Polycell Ltd)

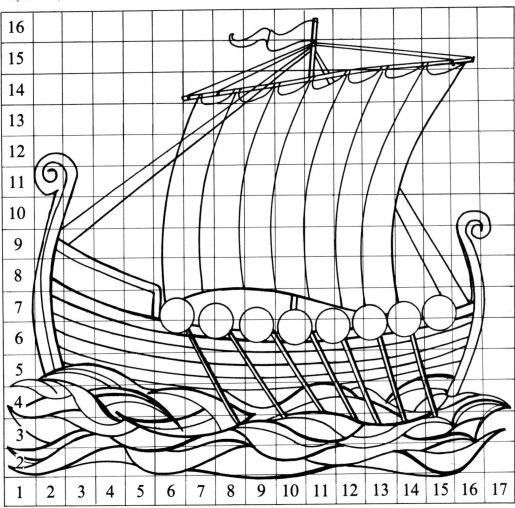

reducing or transferring. Sold by art shops, it consists of a set of flat, adjustable rods, which when guided will produce a design, etc, to a set scale.

PREPARATION AND PRESSING OF FABRICS

Before beginning any stitchery on fabrics, make sure they are free from creases—both background and applied pieces. As fibres in fabrics are so varied, always apply iron heat with caution, testing on a small piece first. Use a damp cloth, on the wrong side of the fabric, if you are uncertain of the reaction.

If fabrics are crease-free when work commences, they will not usually require any further pressing for mounting. Small insignificant creases will disappear when the fabric is stretched over a board. Should work require it, it can be pre-stretched over some damp sheets of newspaper. Place them on a board larger than the work; then, using plenty of drawing pins, pin the fabric over the damp papers, right side up. Leave it to dry naturally.

Soft hangings are more likely to require pressing, especially round the edges. Always press work on the wrong side, avoiding areas with metal threads, beads, etc.

SIGNING AND DATING WORK

It is usually possible to find a convenient place to put your initials and the year of completion on a hanging. Work out a simple way of doing this, with paper and pencil, so that it can be neatly stitched and placed. The thread used should match the hanging, and the stitching should not look obtrusive. It can be done when the hanging is mounted, but requires some ingenuity to dispose of the ends of threads. Alternatively, the details could be added with a fine permanent felt-pen marker.

5 Embroidery Techniques

Wall-hangings can be made from a wide range of techniques and methods, as we have seen, and some very different ones combine well. The most generally used are listed here—specialist books will give more details. Today these techniques are often used experimentally, pushing them beyond the limits accepted in the past, giving endless scope for inventive and creative work.

It is interesting to note how various types of embroidery appeal to people of different temperaments. Although a number of techniques may be explored, embroiderers usually feel attracted to a few specific types of work. If canvas work gives them the greatest satisfaction, they may not feel at home with collage or free stitchery. Conversely, those who prefer the latter may not enjoy blackwork or other counted-thread techniques. It is a mistake, however, to stick too rigidly to one technique—trying out other forms of embroidery is stimulating and encourages imaginative use of them.

APPLIQUÉ

A popular method, suitable for many fabrics and shapes. Appliqué shapes can either have the edges turned under or be left flat, and are sewn down in a number of ways—with couched thread, herringbone stitch, machine stitch, etc. When used on wall-hangings, appliqué has merged into fabric collage.

There are four main points to bear in mind when working appliqué:

1 Try to ensure that the grain of the applied fabric and the background fabric coincide, to reduce risk of puckering.

2 Snip any curved edges that are to be turned under.

3 Do not pull thread tightly when stitching—keep an even tension.

4 Pin or mount the background fabric in a frame, unless it is very large, in which case it should be kept flat on a working surface. Never stitch with the work bunched up in the hand.

Machined Appliqué

Fabrics can be applied by machine, with or without the presser foot. Freer effects are obtained without the presser foot, as in machine embroidery, but practise first. Start with a circle of fabric and pin it to the background, putting the pins at right angles every centimetre. Put the fabric in a ring frame, make it drum-tight, then stitch down, using zig-zag or a free running stitch. Keep the zig-zag close together, working clockwise and removing the pins as you come to them. For a neat finish, the zig-zag should be aligned with the edge of the shape, on the right swing. Otherwise, the edge can be treated freely.

An important point to remember is always to put fabrics in place *before* framing: if they are laid on after the background fabric has been framed, they may bubble when taken out of the frame. (See Machine Embroidery, page 76.)

Machine-appliquéd letters: this method is particularly suited to large letters, for which it is quick and effective. One letter can be worked, using an interesting patterned fabric, or stitch a monogram in a bold colour. Letters with slightly rounded corners are easier; they do not have to be uniform, so try some unconventional shapes.

1 Draw the letter or letters on tracing paper.

2 Do not cut them out, but pin the sheet of paper to the background fabric and carefully stitch on the outline, through paper and fabric, with straight stitch (as in first drawing overleaf).

3 Trim all round, through the paper and fabric, leaving a 5mm border.

4 Remove paper and position letter or letters on fabric. Tack into place and re-stitch on the same line, with straight stitch.

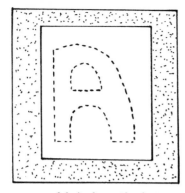

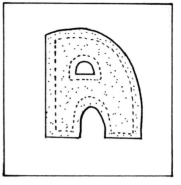

5 Trim away excess fabric from the letters, close to the stitching (as shown in drawing above). Then neaten edge with extra stitching such as zig-zag or satin stitch or a couched thread.

Appliqué on Nets

A delicate soft hanging can be made with shapes of fabric machined on to a net background. Pin and tack them to the net so that they are just touching each other. Stitch them down with zig-zag or satin stitch. Cut away the net for a cutwork effect, or leave it in place, as you prefer. Experiment with shapes—butterflies, flowerheads, whatever comes to mind. Suspend from a narrow rod with loops of thread. A thin, silky fringe could be used, or long tassels.

Reverse Appliqué

Several layers of fabric in different colours are placed together, then carefully cut and stitched to reveal the colours in intricate designs. The Kuna Indians have perfected this technique, using it for making molas, distinctive, blouse-like garments.

It is a technique which is well-suited to making wall-hangings, particularly the soft variety, as the designs are arresting, and the layers of fabric give weight and 'body'. Practise on a small sample first, stitching on a simple design by hand—an apple, for instance.

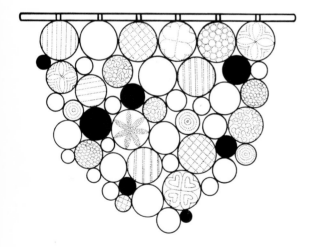

(right) *An apple (originally drawn full-size) to work as a sample. Four layers of fabric are tacked together: green on bottom layer, then brown, then orange, with yellow as top layer. The small triangular shapes are commonly used with this technique*

Personal Approach—Herta Puls

Foreign Influence

Just as canvas, paint and brush can express ideas, so can fabric, thread and needles. The process is perhaps more laborious and needs more dedication.

The greatest influence on my work has been the embroidery of the Kuna Indians. Their molas (blouse-like garments) are worked with great artistry and skill, influenced by their love for their beautiful islands, for saturated bright colours, political thought and most important—deep belief in their traditions and mythology. I was also intrigued with their use of letters as interesting shapes, and incorporation of present-day symbols—even western-style advertisements which they use, sometimes, with no understanding of their meaning.

Their ingenious appliqué technique, which I use in colours and shapes influenced by my own environment, gives a finished overall unity which I find pleasing.

*

The simple shapes of the designs on the colourful molas of the Kuna Indians are formed by careful cutting and stitching through several layers of thin cotton. The technique makes ideal soft hangings and is readily adapted to individual approaches. See also Project 11, page 160

BLACKWORK

A distinctive technique, traditionally worked very finely on dress and household linens. It adapts well to designs for wall-hangings, as the scale of working can be altered by using different fabrics, such as hessian, and a wider range of threads. Metal threads are effective in small amounts, and experiments can be made with other colours too. Blackwork looks dramatic with the colouring reversed—white threads on a black background. Some of the other techniques for wall-hangings combine well with blackwork—appliqué, for example.

Designs should be worked out with careful consideration of the different tones, making some dense and others light. This is achieved by varying the thickness of the thread and the patterns created by the stitches. Geometric patterns can be worked out on graph paper. Several of the design methods discussed in Chapter 2 can be used, for example cut paper, printing, spraying. Black-and-white photographs are a good source of designs, already having obvious tonal areas. Wrought-iron designs can be adapted to blackwork, simply stitched with double running stitch or couching.

Evenweave fabrics should be used and today there is quite a variety of these—linens, monks-

'Knight on Horseback'. A variety of blackwork patterns have been worked to make different tonal areas. The 'chain mail' is particularly effective (Embroiderers' Guild)

'Flower'—machined appliqué. Leaves and petals are cut out in simple shapes, then applied with repeated lines of free-running stitch. By Joy Clucas (English Sewing Ltd)

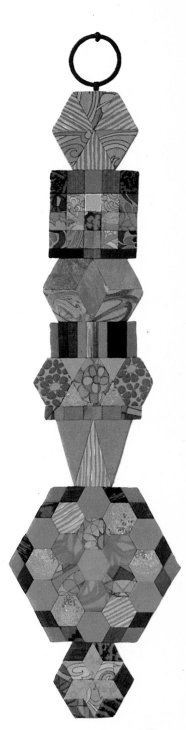

Patchwork hanging: for directions on how to make this, see Project 10, page 159. By Alice Timmins

'*Reconstructed View*'. *An old window-frame from a cottage was restored, including the original catches and hinges. A piece of hand knitting was stretched within the frame and strips of fabric were woven into it. The design is based on a window view in Somerset. By Sian Martin*

Wrought-iron design

cloth, canvas and woollen fabrics, for instance. Paper-backed wall coverings can be used—the stiffness is an advantage for counting the threads and for mounting. Other fabrics should be worked in a frame. Although the traditional blackwork patterns are delightful, it is interesting to make new ones and new textures, especially as they can be adapted to irregular lines and shapes.

Stitches for Blackwork

Whipped back stitch: used for outlining. Work back stitch first, then with another thread in the needle whip over each stitch without entering the fabric.

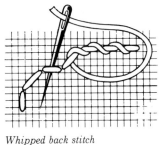

Whipped back stitch

Holbein stitch: also called double running stitch. Working from right to left, work a row of running stitches, over and under three threads of the fabric, following the shape of the design. On the return journey, work in the same way from left to right, filling in the spaces.

Holbein stitch

Honeycomb filling stitch: work from the top downwards. Bring the needle through at the arrow, then insert it four threads to the right (A). Bring the needle through at B, insert again at A, and back to B. Insert at C (four threads to the left) and bring through at D. To work the next row, turn the fabric round and work in the same way. Where the rows connect, the vertical stitches are worked into the same holes.

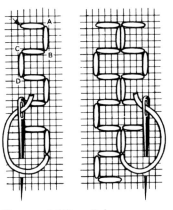

Honeycomb filling stitch

Wave stitch filling: work from right to left. Bring thread through at arrow. Insert needle four threads up and two to the right, at A. Bring through at B (four threads to the left). Insert at arrow, then bring through at C, four threads to the left. Turn the fabric round to commence the second row. Work into the same holes as shown, to produce diamond shapes.

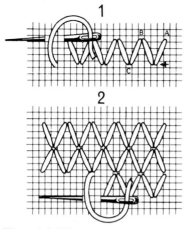

Wave stitch filling

Ringed back stitch: work from right to left. Bring needle through at arrow, insert at A, three threads down, bring through at B—six threads up and three to the left. Insert at arrow, bring through at C (three threads up and six to the left). Insert needle at B, bringing it through at D (three threads down and six to the left). Insert needle at C, bringing it through at E (six threads down and three to the left). Turn the fabric round for the second stage. All connecting stitches are worked into the same holes.

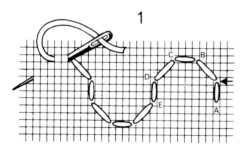

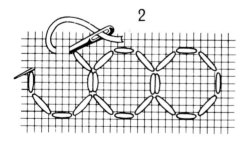

Ringed back stitch

CANVAS WORK

There are two main types of canvas, single and double weave. They are measured by the number of threads to the inch, and can be very fine or as coarse as rug canvas. Mounting the work in a frame will prevent distortion but is not essential for coarse rug canvas.

Although woollen threads have a natural affinity with canvas many other threads can be used—such as raffia, crochet threads, fabric strips, etc. Usually the whole canvas is covered, but parts of it can be left uncovered as part of the design. Canvas combines well with a number of techniques and experimental methods, and hangs well so is excellent on walls. Or small areas of canvas can be worked separately and applied to other backgrounds.

A number of different stitches are associated with canvas work, giving variety in textures and patterns. Many of them transfer well to other fabrics, including the stitches based on cross stitch.

A rose garland from the Longleat Tree wall-hanging (shown on page 9). The roses are worked in petit point (tent) stitch in two shades of red, highlighted in pink. The canvas background has been left unworked, but could be stitched later if desired. Made up as a framed panel (Longleat Press Office)

Canvas-work Stitches

Petit-point stitch: bring the thread out on the left-hand side, on the top part of the first stitch; pass the needle down diagonally over the crossed threads of the canvas, then under two threads. The second row is worked from right to left, the needle passing the crossed threads up and over, then under two threads. All stitches should slope in the same direction.

 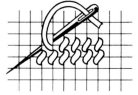

Petit-point stitch

Double cross stitch: work a single cross stitch, then bring the needle through the fabric, between the lower crossed threads (A). Insert the needle centrally, above the crossed threads, bringing it out, centrally, to the left (B). Insert the needle on the opposite side, vertically, and bring through fabric, ready for next stitch (C).

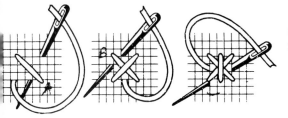

Double cross stitch

Rice stitch: work a row of cross stitch, then with a contrasting thread (sometimes thinner) work a diagonal stitch across over each corner.

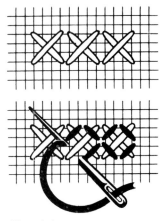

Rice stitch

Long-legged cross stitch: work from left to right, take a long slanting stitch, bringing needle out vertically a short distance below (A). Insert needle above, halfway along slanting stitch, then bring it out vertically through the fabric, under the slanting stitch, level with A.

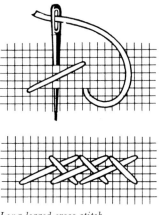

Long-legged cross stitch

Norwich stitch: has a fascinating three-dimensional appearance, when worked, which makes it very suitable for wall-hangings. Can be worked singly, or in blocks. Although the diagram may look complicated, it is not difficult to do, once it has been practised a few times and the sequence of working is understood.

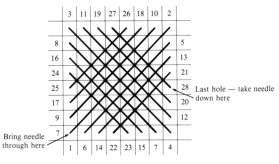

Norwich stitch

COLLAGE

A rewarding method to use; so many interpretations are possible, with few rules to follow. Although the literal meaning is 'to stick', collage has now come to mean the bringing together of a selection of fabrics, threads, beads and other

71

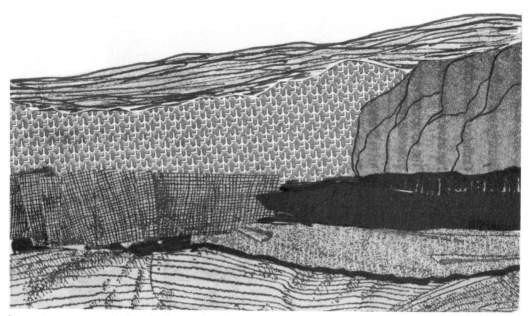

items to express a design. It is nearly always worked on a background, though not necessarily textile.

Applied fabrics can be attached in a wide variety of ways, and neatened or not as required, using hand or machine sewing.

Although collages are more satisfactory when stitched, adhesives can be used on some areas, depending on the design: they are particularly useful for fixing awkward pieces, such as a bird's beak or a face. It is not always possible to pierce a glued fabric with a needle, the exception being where PVA adhesives are used. (Small amounts of these adhesives are also useful to hold fabrics in place temporarily.) A stitched collage has a softer, more pliable appearance than one which has been glued.

Collage designs can be worked freely straight on to fabric, or a drawing of the main outlines can be made. If doing this, make two tracings—one to cut up for patterns, the other as a check for your positioning. Background fabrics should be carefully chosen, allowing at least 5cm for mounting. Cut out fabric pieces, put them in position, pin and tack them. Finish the edges as suits the design—stitching, couching, covering with braids. Beads and other collage items can be added. If the finished design is to be put under glass, the edges of the fabric need not be treated, as the glass will hold them in place. (See 'Butterfly', Project 1, page 146.)

Collage designs can be created with strips of fabric that have been pleated, ruched, gathered, etc. The fabrics should be selected to give a good range; chiffon, corduroy, velvet, plastic mesh and nets were used to interpret this landscape, which relies also on a subtle blend of colours to achieve its effect. The fabrics should be pinned to their background, then caught down, keeping the stitches unobtrusive. An outer window mount of card, and a wooden frame, glazed, give a good finish

*

Personal Approach—Richard Box

A Series of Approaches
I like to understand and explore a subject fully, before I actually commence a collage, so I usually make a series of studies beforehand in other media—water-colours, pastels and oil paints. Working on several studies at the same time helps to isolate different aspects of the subject, such as growth patterns, colours and tones, lines and shapes, and how they relate to each other.

At the start of a collage, I draw on to a background fabric (usually hessian) the essential structure of the composition, using crayons and felt pens. Then, from a vast selection of all types of materials, I select the relevant colours and textures, to suit the idea which has emerged from previous paintings and drawings. They are cut into shapes, and stuck on to the background with Marvin Medium.

The collage is machine stitched, with the darner foot, using coloured sewing cottons. This integrates the colours, and gives more detailed delineation. Finally, the collage is handstitched, with a variety of other threads to give a greater degree of texture and colour.

Richard Box's 'Delphiniums', collage with hundreds of tiny pieces of fabric in delphinium colours stitched by machine to the background, with some hand stitching and textured threads added. One of a series of flower studies

*

COUCHING

A quick method for working a bold, continuous line, covering edges or filling areas. A thick thread, or group of threads, is placed on the surface of the fabric, then held down with a finer thread which matches or contrasts with it. The stitch can be either unobtrusive or decorative, and can be worked by hand or machine.

Raw edges of fabric shapes can be effectively concealed with a couched thread, selecting from the vast range available. A number of threads can be placed together and held down with various stitches, and experiments should be made to try out different effects. For example, if a thick line of thread is made with twenty-four single strands of Anchor stranded cotton, and held down with a single strand of coton-á-broder, using a small, firm, straight stitch, fairly close together, it produces a surprising 'beaded' effect, which is used a great deal on professional ecclesiastical work, for edging appliqué shapes. It is worked in a frame for an even result (See banner, page 123).

Couching is used extensively in goldwork.

73

CUTWORK

Traditional embroidery shows a number of different types of cutwork: portions of the background fabric are carefully cut away to form the design. Today, fabric is cut away in freer style, creating intriguing designs and exploiting the effects of depth that can be obtained by using several layers of fabrics, one over the other, with different spaces removed.

Cutwork can be worked by hand or machine, using buttonhole stitch, whipping, zig-zag or close satin stitch. It is easier to work the stitching and *then* cut away the fabric. This will help keep the spaces from pulling out of shape.

If working by hand, mark the spaces to be removed with tacking thread (pencil, etc, could be used if it will not be seen). A row of running stitches (A) can be worked first, to act as padding under the stitching. Buttonhole bars can be worked to link shapes. Take two threads across, then buttonhole them, keeping the bar detached from the fabric except at each end (B). Buttonhole the shape, keeping the looped edge to the inside (C). Then cut away the unwanted fabric.

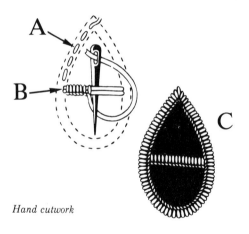

Hand cutwork

Eyelets, very small holes, can be worked differently. Mark the circle, then run a row of stitches round it. Pierce the centre with a stiletto or other tool such as a thick knitting needle, and push the ragged edge under. Closely overcast the folded edge and running stitch it. Larger holes can be made by cutting across their centre and folding under the raw edges. If a very large cut shape is required, the cut edges can be strengthened with wire, etc, in the folded edge.

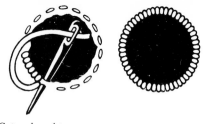

Cutwork eyelets

Machined Cutwork

Mark on the fabric the shapes to be removed, but do not cut them until a strengthening of stitching has been worked. Frame the fabric, then run a few lines of straight stitches round the marked areas. Make the lines as close as possible, and the stitches as small as possible—this will prevent the edges of the hole from stretching, and the work going out of shape. Cut the fabric away, inside the stitching, quite close to it. Stitch across the cut shape, in any direction; then work patterns on the web of thread. Neaten the edges of the shape with satin stitch, couched thread, etc.

Spaces can be decorated with woven wheels, needle-weaving, beads, and so on. Machine embroidery combines well with cutwork, and with practice can be used to make decorative fillings.

Other fabrics can be placed behind the spaces, giving scope for using different textures and colours.

DRAWN THREAD

Some of the threads are withdrawn from the fabric, usually in horizontal and vertical bands. The remaining threads are grouped together with decorative stitchery, and where an open space occurs it is filled in with woven wheels or a lacy filling. Of peasant origin, the technique has been used extensively in the past for decorating household linens, church vestments and dress.

Drawn-thread work has a light lacy appearance, and experiments can be made on different fabrics, eg hessian or scrims, with a variety of threads. Beads, rings and so on could be incorporated. It is a useful technique to use in one area of a design—or small pieces can be worked and then appliquéd on.

Drawn-thread Stitches

Stitches associated with drawn thread can be adapted for other forms of embroidery, particularly where long threads are incorporated or an open mesh fabric is used.

Ladder hemstitch: this pulls the threads into clearly defined groups. Bring needle through fabric (A), then insert it a short distance above, passing it behind the required number of threads and bringing it up. Insert it again, over the same threads, and bring it out just below them (B). Repeat at the opposite end of the threads (C).

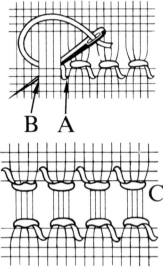

'Orange Slice', a machined cutwork panel, in satin stitch on furnishing dupion. It is mounted over canvas-work stitchery, on hessian, giving it a three-dimensional quality. By Jane Blair (Charles Risk)

Interlaced hemstitch: worked on a basis of ladder stitch, but this can be omitted. Secure another thread (which can be thicker and contrasting). Pass the needle over the first group and insert from left to right under the second group, with the first group under the needle (A). Twist the second group over, so that the needle is pointing to the left (B). Pull thread through. A bead, etc, can be put on the thread.

Ladder hemstitch

Zig-zag hemstitch: a variation of ladder stitch, using an even number of threads. The first row is worked as in ladder stitch, but the second row starts by pulling only half of the first group of threads, which are then pulled together with half of the next group.

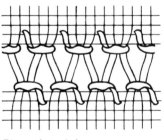

Zig-zag hemstitch

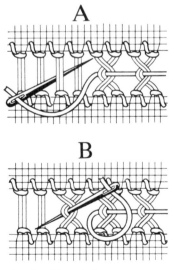

Interlaced hemstitch

GOLDWORK

A specialised form of surface decoration, different metal threads being couched to form the design. It sometimes incorporates gold kid, suede, etc, beads, sequins and other bits and pieces. It is most often used for ecclesiastical work, and although it is expensive it is a durable and rich form of decoration. It can be used with great effect in small areas of a design, or the metal threads can be used to outline shapes, etc.

There are many different types of metal thread available, of varying thickness and texture. It is advisable to frame the work carefully for satisfactory results. If you are not familiar with goldwork, look at a specialist book before beginning.

MACHINE EMBROIDERY

Simple or intricate effects, delicate or dramatic, can be worked once you have had some practice, and machine embroidery combines well with other techniques. Pieces can be worked separately and then applied to a design. Always mount the fabric in a frame—it *must* be really taut for good results. The teeth on the machine are lowered and both hands used to guide the frame.

Framing for Machine Embroidery

The inner ring should be bound with tape or bias binding as in the left-hand drawing below to ensure a good grip on the fabric and to prevent it becoming marked. Keep the tape in one length and wind it round tightly, securing the ends with a few stitches on the inside of the ring.

Frame the fabric flat, on a clean surface, standing up to do it. Lay down the outer ring, then put the fabric over it, right side up; then press the inner ring into the fabric and outer ring (upper righthand drawing below). Adjust the screw on the outer ring so that a firm push is needed to insert the inner one. Tighten the fabric by pulling upwards and inwards, the palms of your hands resting on the frame to stop the fabric becoming dislodged. Keep the warp and weft threads straight. Tighten the screw, with a small screwdriver if necessary. Work the machine embroidery with the frame uppermost, as seen in the upper righthand drawing.

Beginning Machine Embroidery

Again, if you are new to this spend a little time practising before beginning a design on the final fabric.

1 Thread the machine with Sylko 40 or 50. Machine embroidery thread may be used instead—preferably 50 in the bobbin, where a fine thread is advisable. If this is also used in the needle, loosen the tension slightly. If the top thread snaps, it is because the tension is too tight.

2 Use a 90/14 needle—a finer needle may break.

3 Remove the presser foot and holding screw.

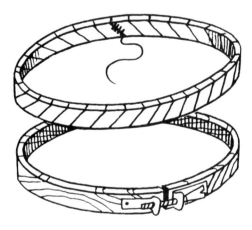

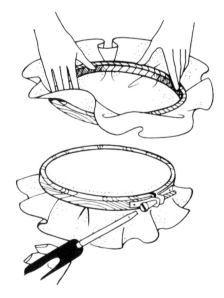

4 Drop or cover the feed as directed in the darning section of the instruction book.

5 Until you are experienced, use a darning foot. Many embroiderers work without it, but catching your finger is a hazard; plastic finger-shields can be bought for a few pence. Insert the framed fabric under the needle.

6 Draw the bobbin thread up on to the fabric by holding the fabric firmly with the left fore-finger, then turning the needle by hand, allowing plenty of cotton in the needle. Pull on the top thread, and the bottom thread will come to the top.

7 Turn the needle down into the hole through which the bottom thread has come and hold both ends under your left forefinger, pressing down on the fabric.

8 Lower the presser foot bar. This must be done—it engages the top tension. It is also important to hold down the threads until machining has begun, or they may snarl and clog the machine.

9 Run the machine medium-fast, moving the frame smoothly in a series of circles, squares, etc. Do not work slowly; fluency comes with the machine working at a fair speed and smoothly.

10 To move from one place to another, lift the needle from the fabric and lift the presser bar foot to remove the top thread tension. Move the frame to the required place, dip the needle down into the work, *lower the presser foot* and continue.

11 When some control has been achieved, try machining with the zig-zag stitch. This will give different effects: if a narrow stitch is used and the frame moved slowly, a solid line results (free satin stitch). Using the widest zig-zag, the effect can be varied according to whether the frame is moved backwards and forwards or sideways.

Stretchy and flimsy materials which do not hold their shape when cut, eg chiffons and nylon hosiery, give subtle and delicate effects to a design. The easiest way to deal with them is to mark the shape required on the background fabric, frame it, then pin the flexible fabric over the shape and beyond it. Free machine-stitch round the edge of the shape several times. Cut away the surplus fabric close to the stitching. Extra stitching can be added if required.

NEEDLE-WEAVING

This used to be a formal method, used for decorating dress and household linens. Thread is woven over and under on a drawn-thread base, or else on a base of threads stitched into the fabric. Today the method is used on a wide range of fabrics in a much freer and more experimental way (see 'Shady Glade', page 135 and 'Green Rondels', page 79). It can be worked in any shape or area, with a variety of different threads: most effective are threads with a slight sheen. It can also be worked without fabric—the long threads can be attached to the edge of a rigid support such as a lampshade ring or other type of frame (as in 'Green Rondels').

When working with fabric, use a frame—a picture frame, artist's stretchers or a tambour frame (for small areas). The base threads will then be held taut for your weaving. Use a blunt needle.

Areas can be worked solidly or made to look lacy or spiky. Beads, rings, etc can easily be incorporated, and needle-weaving can be super-imposed on other stitching. Interesting base threads can be formed by withdrawing every other thread, in both directions. Practise on a coarse fabric such as hessian. A three-dimensional effect can be obtained which looks intriguing (see 'Pear' photograph, page 142).

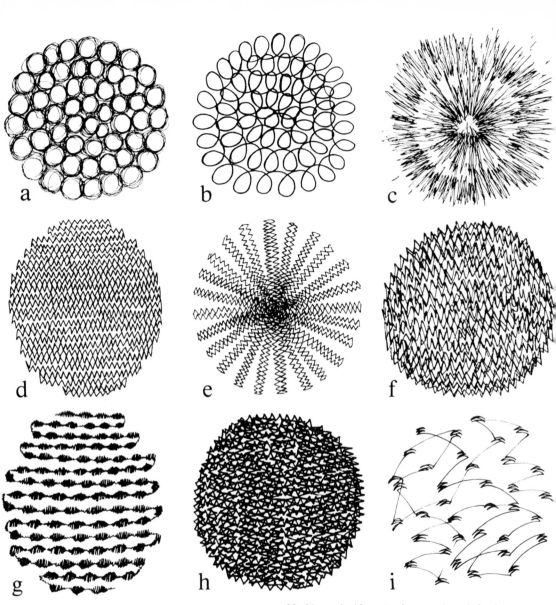

Machine embroidery: (a) free running stitch—four lines of stitching round each circle (b) the same stitch worked in a continuous circular motion (c) free running stitch radiating out from the centre of the circle (d) free zig-zag, worked backwards and forwards to produce an even all-over texture (e) free zig-zag radiating out from the centre (f) overall texture produced with zig-zag, moving the frame in circles (g) free zig-zag stitch, moving the frame backwards and forwards while opening and closing the stitch-width control (h) zig-zag worked in one direction, the work then being turned and the stitch worked again, on top, in the other direction (i) satin-stitch 'beads' worked freely to produce an overall texture (see also Project 17, page 171) (English Sewing Ltd)

Machine-stitched letters, formed with zig-zag, satin and straight stitches

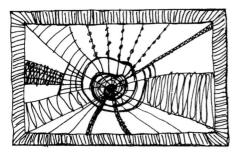

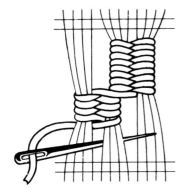

Needleweaving

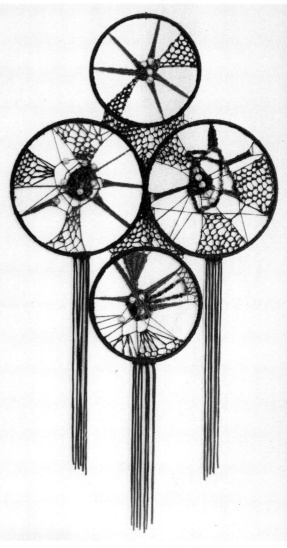

'Green Rondels'. Lampshade rings have been blanket stitched with shiny olive-green crochet thread, then strung across and filled with needleweaving and knotted buttonhole filling. A textured chenille wool, in variegated greens and orange, has been woven into some of the rings, and green glass beads add interest. Tubular rayon has been used for the long narrow fringes; loose ends should be carefully run into the edge of the ring at the back, down into the needleweaving, or into the centre at the back

Any of the bases mentioned can also be worked with buttonhole or whipped stitch, combined with needle-weaving or used on their own. Rope-like, linear effects result, which are suitable for designs based on fruit, trees, cellular constructions, and so on.

Net darning, using a variety of threads, based on a wax crayon rubbing, 'Wood Knot'. Threads are taken to each side to start and finish, then sandwiched between two cut-out circles of very thin plywood. When glued together the circles warped, giving an unusual effect.

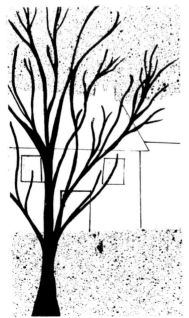

NET EMBROIDERY

Tulle and synthetic nets are surprisingly strong, and stitches worked on them look light and delicate; they are particularly effective with the sun shining through them. The working thread should be as long as possible, to avoid joins, which must be made as neatly as possible. In a small design, the ends of the threads could be arranged on either side of the fabric and then enclosed by the frame or mount.

Linear patterns, with flowing lines, are quick to work, using a simple darning stitch; but many other stitches can be used.

Another method with nets is to build up several layers, cutting away some parts to give a variation of colours. This combines well with machine stitching.

Irish Carrickmacross embroidery combines a fine, thin material with net; the two are placed together, and then designs—usually floral—are stitched, using an outline of thin cord; unwanted portions of top fabric are then cut away, revealing the net background. It is an excellent technique for the sewing-machine and can be used to make delicate-looking hangings.

PATCHWORK

The enthusiastic revival of interest in patchwork has brought forth many new approaches ideal for use on wall-hangings. Fabrics of different colours, tones and textures are cut into shapes and stitched together. Geometric shapes are most often used, but any shape may be fitted together provided a pattern of the design is made beforehand and the pieces are cut accurately from templates made from card, plastic or metal for durability.

The fabrics are tacked on to the shape, then stitched together. If the templates are paper, they are then removed from the work; using templates of one of the various types of Vilene gives the finished work extra firmness and has the advantage that they can be left in it. Patches can be sewn by hand or machine, and whole backgrounds formed from small pieces, on which stitchery can be added. Units of patches can be made separately, then joined together to give

(left) *Machining on net. Outlines can be stitched on net in a straight stitch, using a dark thread, and placed over a background. If the net matches the background fabric, the dark stitching will appear to be superimposed on the design*

hangings of unusual shapes (see Project 10, page 159).

Geometric patterns can give striking designs, particularly if the colours are carefully planned—graph paper is helpful. The finished effect can be enhanced by designing the top and bottom edges and the method of suspension (see Chapter 8) in conjunction with the templates used.

The popular 'log cabin' arrangement, made up of strips round a centre square, gives considerable scope for experiment. Small blocks can be joined together, with interest added by colour planning; if half the strips are light and half are dark, striking patterns are formed. The 'log cabin' formation can also be used to make one large hanging, with the centre square as the focal point. This pattern can be stitched by hand or machine. Make up a small sample block so that you understand the method and possible effects.

The outer shape of this patchwork panel echoes the smaller inner triangles of which the panel is composed. Even the clowns are constructed from triangles; a beautifully made gypsy peg-doll is an unexpected focal point. The different colours of machine embroidery cotton used for the clowns' hair were also used for a twisted cord to finish the edge of the panel. By Belinda Fairclough (Terry Waddington)

Log Cabin Patchwork

1 Mark out a 19cm square of firm cotton, then *tear* it from the larger piece to ensure it is straight on the grain. Pull it into a square, then fold it diagonally to mark its centre. Cut a piece of dark fabric 3cm square, and stitch it exactly in the centre of the cotton square, close to the edges.

2 Cut long strips of fabrics, 3cm wide, along the straight of the grain. Sort into light and dark colours. There is no need to cut the strips into lengths—stitch them to the base, then cut off as

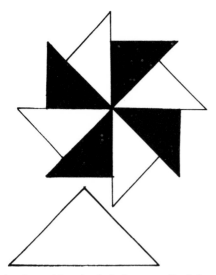

A triangle, used imaginatively for an appliqué shape

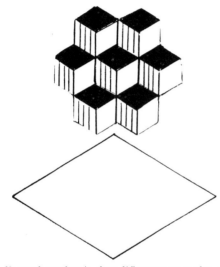

A diamond template in three different tones makes a three-dimensional-looking box pattern

required. Stitch a light piece to the bottom edge of the patch, and cut it off level with the patch.

3 Press the first strip down, then stitch a dark strip to the left of it, trimming level with the patch and the first strip.

4 Press a dark strip down, then stitch another dark strip to the top of the square patch and across the trimmed edge of the first dark strip. Trim level.

5 Stitch a light strip to the right side of the square patch. Trim level.

6 Continue in the same sequence until the base is covered.

Variations: very thin fabrics can be cut double width, folded and then stitched down with two edges placed together.

Ribbons and braids can be stitched directly into place, having no raw edge.

One large square can be formed, using a piece of embroidery—eg canvas work—for the centre.

Thick and thin strips look effective: the formation square will become off-centre.

The 'log cabin' of strips can be used to make a mount for panels.

PULLED WORK

This is also known as 'drawn fabric', but as the threads of the fabric are pulled together to make different patterns, 'pulled work' is more apt—and less likely to be confused with drawn-thread work. It has been a popular embroidery technique for centuries, with devotees in many countries. Originally worked on fine linens, it is used with renewed vigour today on any fabric

Jigsaw shapes are unusual for patchwork, and would be an enjoyable pattern for those who like a challenge. The design could be made completely from jigsaw-shaped pieces or these could be used merely as a border

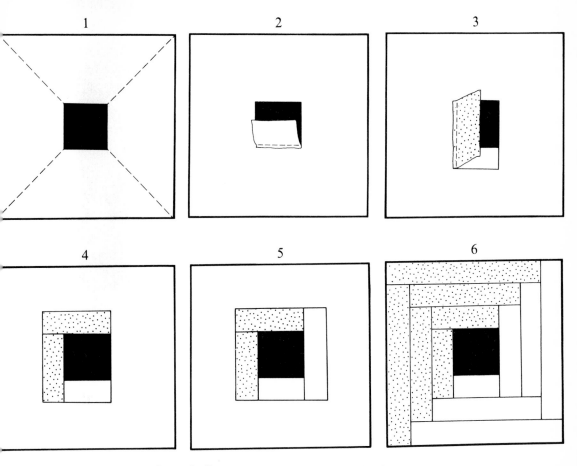

1

2

3

4

5

6

Log-cabin patchwork

with a loose weave—scrims of all types are favourites.

It is not necessary to work in a frame, but as some loose fabrics fray badly it is easier to pin the fabric to a picture frame—not tautly, as there must be enough 'give' to pull the threads in the required direction.

Pulled-work Stitches

Although a number of stitches have evolved especially for pulled work, a satisfactory design can be worked from just three of them: four-sided stitch, eyelets and satin stitch. The thread, traditionally, has been colour-matched to the fabric so as not to detract from the patterns made by the stitches, and even today this 'rule' is usually followed, though interesting experiments can be made with coloured and textured threads.

Beads, rings, etc, can be successfully incorporated. Colour can also be introduced by mounting the embroidery over a different-coloured fabric, to show through the spaces. Small pieces can be worked separately, and applied to a design.

These stitches are particularly suited to mesh fabrics but adaptable to others.

Four-sided stitch: if to be worked with a regular appearance, the same number of threads are counted each time, eg four. Bring the needle through the fabric, then insert four threads above (A), bring it through at B, pulling the thread tightly. Insert (needle) where thread first emerged (arrowed) bringing it out at C. Insert needle at A and bring out at B. Continue in this way pulling thread firmly. For other rows, turn work round.

For use on firmer fabrics, the thread is not pulled tightly but left to form a squared filling.

Eyelets: straight stitches are worked over a square, all entering the same central hole. This

83

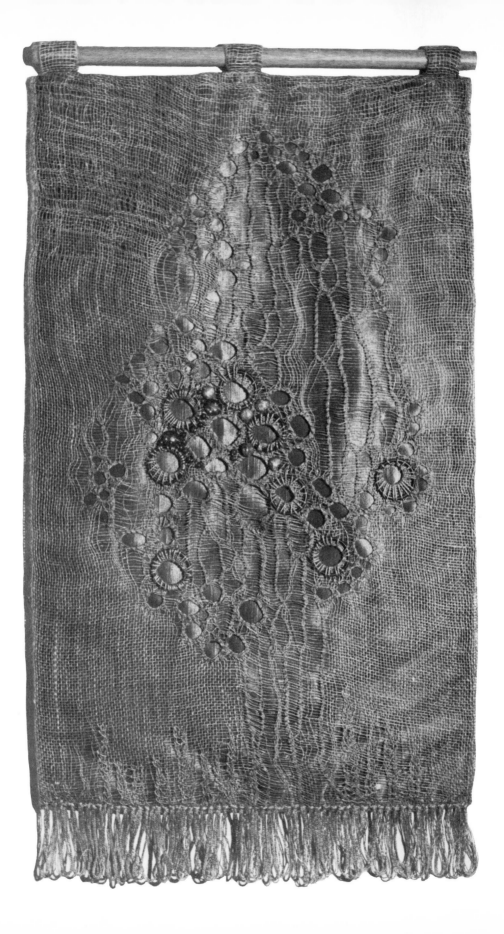

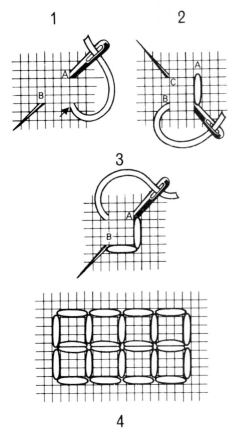

1   2

3

4

Four-sided stitch

Star eyelet

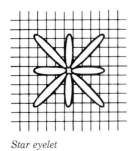

(left) *Soft hanging in pulled work on plasterer's scrim, with curtain-rings and beads. Mounted over a bright golden shiny furnishing fabric and backed with calico. The soft fawn thread used to stitch the rings is also used to make the fringe in velvet stitch*

eyelet can be worked in many different ways, pulled tightly so that the stitches whip the fabric, and make a larger hole. More stitches can be worked, making a circular or squared eyelet. On firmer fabrics, the stitches can be left to form the pattern. Part of the eyelet could be woven, or edged with small beads, etc.

Pin stitch: bring through the fabric as at A, insert needle at B, bring out at C. Insert again at B, bring out at C, twice to form a double stitch. Bring out at D. Pull stitches firmly. Can be used in drawn-thread work, and for applying a firm fabric to a mesh.

QUILTING

An ancient technique, used to add warmth and decoration to clothing and bedding. It is still much in evidence today for the same purpose, but in addition the decorative and relief effects are being exploited for making wall-hangings. The three-dimensional look can be subtle, as in some wadded quilting designs, or very pronounced—achieved with the stuffed method. The different varieties of quilting give scope for experimental work, especially as a wide range of fabrics can be used. Fabrics with a sheen can be stitched to take advantage of the play of light. Velvet gives some interesting effects, especially when it is machined.

All the quilting methods can be carried out by hand or machine, or both. Stitches are usually running or back stitch—chain stitch is also effective.

There are four main types of quilting:

Flat quilting: has no interlining or padding, and consists of two layers of fabric only. It is used mainly to work decorative stitching and also to give extra weight to a top fabric. It is particularly suited to wall-hangings, and to machine stitching.

Wadded quilting (also known as English quilting): a layer of wadding is placed between top and bottom fabric. (Thin foam could be tried—it gives a springier appearance.) The stitching is used to make patterns on the top fabric, simply or intricately. (See 'Brown Owl', Project 8, page 156.)

Corded (Italian) quilting: again two layers of fabric are used. The work is stitched with distinctive parallel lines, placed close together, making channels. These are threaded (on the back of the work) with thick wool, piping cord,

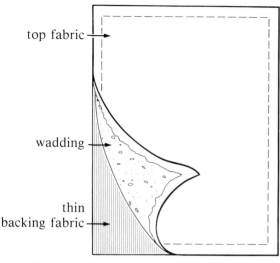

top fabric

wadding

thin backing fabric

Wadded quilting

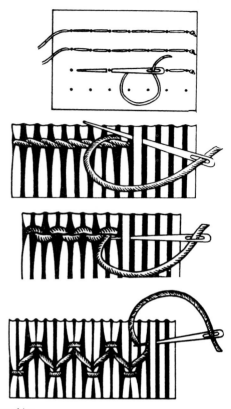

Smocking

etc, to make a raised line. Patterns are linear in character, and look best on fabrics which have a slight sheen—satin or taffeta, for example. Experiments could be made using clear plastic tubing, stitching the channels on either side of it, producing a pronounced raised line.

Stuffed (Trapunto) quilting: this can be used on a wide variety of designs, to give a more pronounced three-dimensional appearance than any of the other methods. Two fabrics are tacked together (a), then the design is stitched, mounted in a frame (b). The under fabric is slit, selected areas are stuffed with wadding, kapok, etc (c). The gap is then closed with overcasting stitches (d). This method can be incorporated with other types of quilting and also different embroidery techniques.

SMOCKING
Although traditional smocking, used on clothing, has a recognisable uniformity, due to the method of forming gathers in the fabric, a freer approach can be used for wall-hangings. Several folds can be stitched together, leaving other parts unstitched; gathers can be stitched in interesting cellular patterns, which could be worked separately and then applied to your design.

Fabric is drawn up by gathering, picking up a tiny portion of fabric, from regularly spaced dots. A transfer can be bought or a pattern used on a ready-printed fabric. The transfer should be

ironed on to the back of the fabric. Complete the stitches for the depth of fabric required before drawing up (as in the first drawing). Then pull the fabric into gathers by pulling the loose end of cotton on each row. Tie the ends together in pairs.

Then work the smocking stitches on the right side. Some of the traditional stitches, stem, cable or honeycomb, as shown, can be used experimentally. Beads, braids and cords can be added for extra texture. Pieces of tie-dyed fabric can be smocked separately and then added to a design—the random patterns give unusual effects.

Hand-quilted panel, 'Fire Thistle', with extra padding in the centre, worked on flame-coloured furnishing fabric. Gold and bronze threads give a rich effect, and glass, pearl and bugle beads are added. The textured wool, stitched in knotted cable chain, has a maroon chenille wool couched on either side of it and the same colour has been used for the outer fabric mount, giving an unusual colour scheme. The wooden outer frame has been sprayed with gold paint. (Ian Robson)

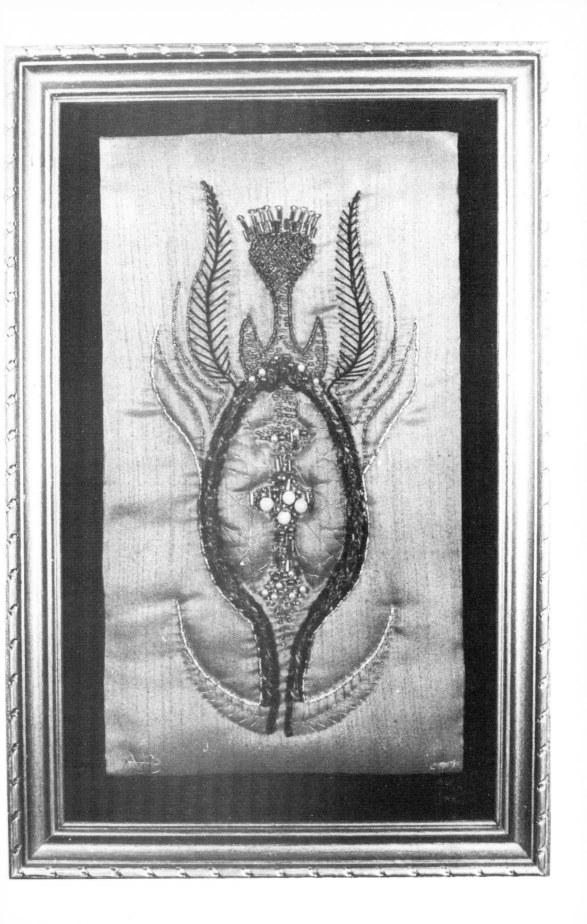

6 Stitches

It is not always realised that there are a tremendous number of different stitches and each is capable of creating a fascinating variety of patterns. When threads, too, are varied, a richly textured work can result. The scale, also, can be altered to suit the design and size of hanging. It is not necessary to be able to work a great number of stitches—a limited number, worked freely, can give vitality, and it is challenging to work a design in one stitch, varying the threads and the stitch itself.

In the past, stitches had to be chosen with care to suit the use of the article being made, especially if it required frequent laundering. There is far greater freedom when stitching wall-hangings, and experiments made with stitches can give much enjoyment both to the worker and the beholder.

Starting sewing: the ends of the thread should be made secure, and there are several different ways of doing this, depending on the fabrics and method used. If starting on a plain background, knot the thread, insert the needle a short distance away, and bring the needle up at the starting point of the stitching, leaving the knot lying temporarily on top of the fabric. The knot can be snipped off later, and the end threaded into existing stitching.

The fabric should be taken into account—if it is thick and closely woven, knots are not likely to make any impression on the surface, so they can be used on the underside, if more convenient. But if the fabric is thin, then more care should be taken—a tiny double stitch to begin and end the thread could be used, running the ends into the back of the work. When ending a thread, never cut off close to the last stitch, as the thread would work loose.

On thin fabrics: problems of working on a thin background fabric can be partly overcome by backing with a thin lining material, if it suits the method. Tack the fabrics together with their grains matching, and work in a frame to keep them flat. This double layer conceals threads and gives strength to the top layer.

BASIC STITCHES

Stitches can be used to secure fabrics to each other, to neaten raw edges, to make surface decoration and to create textures.

Basic stitches—running stitch, stem stitch, chain stitch, herringbone stitch and blanket stitch—can be used for all types of work. It is important to know these basic stitches, and to experiment with them as required. Try out different ways of creating an effect, using a variety of threads. It will be noticed that some stitches look better in a thin thread than a thick one, and vice-versa. It is often difficult to visualise how a stitch will look when worked, so experiment as much as possible, having no inhibitions about straight lines!

When learning a stitch, there are two points to bear in mind: follow the correct direction of working (to left or right) until familiar with it; and, if the stitch will not 'come right' look carefully at the instructions, and observe where the needle should be in relation to the thread—ie under or over it?

Running stitch: pass the needle under and over the fabric. Usually the upper stitches are of even length, with the under stitch smaller, but for wall-hangings the stitch can be worked either evenly or irregularly. It is used a great deal in hand quilting. It can be laced—used as a basis for threading with a different colour.

Stem stitch: work from left to right, slanting the needle slightly, along a line. This stitch is extremely useful as a filling or outline stitch, and is very quick to work.

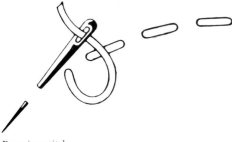

Running stitch

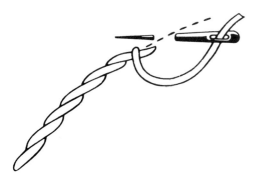

Laced running stitch

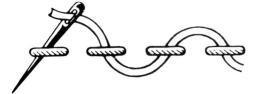

Stem stitch

Chain stitch

Herringbone stitch: to work regularly, stitch between two parallel lines, either imagined or marked. Working from left to right, bring the needle out on the lower line and insert it on the upper line, taking a small stitch to the left, with the thread hanging below the needle. Next, insert the needle on the lower line, a little to the right, and take a small stitch to the left, with the thread above the needle.

This is another very versatile stitch—it can be used to neaten a raw edge; fill a space; create texture and pattern, when worked irregularly; act as a couching stitch; or be threaded with a variety of different colours. It is worked closer together for shadow work.

Chain stitch: bring thread through fabric, hold it down with left thumb, then insert needle back where it emerged, bringing it up again, a short distance away. Pull the needle through, keeping the thread under the needle, forming a loop. Do not pull tightly. This is a neat, attractive stitch, with a wide variety of uses—to form lines (which can be backstitched) to fill a shape with shading, to make patterns, or to disguise the raw edges of applied fabric. Work one row just inside the raw edge and another just beyond it, on the background fabric. Lace the two inner sides of the stitches together with a matching thread, pulling them over the raw edge.

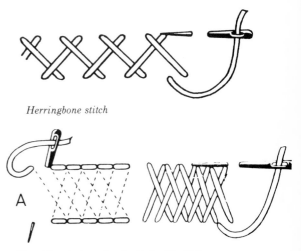

Herringbone stitch

Closed herringbone (or double back) stitch

Blanket stitch: to work regularly, stitch on two parallel lines, marked or imagined. Bring the needle out on the lower line (working from left to right), insert it on the top line, to the right. Bring it out on the bottom line, keeping the needle straight, and over the thread. Pull through gently, to form a loop. If worked close together it is known as buttonhole stitch (righthand drawing). This stitch is used extensively and is capable of infinite variation.

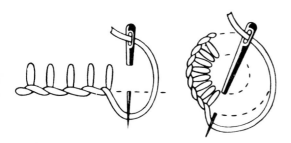

Blanket stitch and buttonhole stitch

OTHER STITCHES

Back stitch: bring the needle through the fabric, then take a small stitch backwards, bringing the needle through again, in front of the thread. The next stitch is made where the needle first emerged, and so on. Back stitch can be used instead of running stitch, in quilting, and forming shapes for padding. It can be used to form lines, and as a basis for threading and whipping.

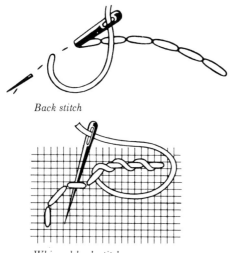

Back stitch

Whipped back stitch

Pekinese stitch: loop another thread, matching or contrasting, on a basis of back stitch. The needle should only enter the fabric at the beginning and end of the stitch. The loops are shown open in the diagram, but should be pulled a little more as it is worked.

Pekinese stitch

Satin stitch: straight stitches are worked close together to fill a shape. The stitches should not be too long, and look effective worked slanting. A raised effect can be achieved by working running stitch first.

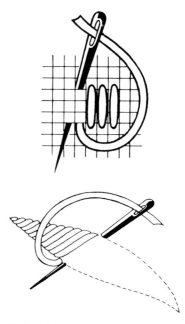

Satin stitch

Long and short stitch: only the first row of stitches are different lengths—make them alternately long and short. Working backwards and forwards, along the rows, alternately, make the other rows of stitches of equal size, but interlocking into the row above. It gives scope for shaded effects, and is a useful filling stitch.

Long and short stitch

Sheaf stitch: groups of satin stitch are tied in the centre with overcasting stitch. Bring the needle up centrally, then to one side, to make the overcasting. Replace the needle where it emerged.

Sheaf stitch

Scroll stitch: bring the needle through the fabric, loop the thread to the right, then insert the needle inside the loop, taking a small slanting stitch to the left. The thread should be under the needle. Pull needle through gently.

Cretan stitch: bring the needle through the fabric (A). Hold the thread upwards, insert the needle on the lower line, pointing it inward (B). Taking a small portion of thread, bring the needle through (C). Insert the needle on the top line (D), and bring it through, taking a small portion of fabric, with the thread under the needle.

This is a simple stitch to work, and very effective for free-stitchery. It can be varied by making the stitches different lengths, and working it closely or widely spaced. It is one of the few stitches which look as effective worked in a very fine thread as in a medium or thick one.

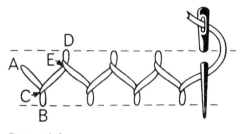

Cretan stitch

Fly stitch: bring the thread through the fabric at top left, hold it down with your thumb; insert the needle to the right, on the same level, then bring it out equidistant between the two points, underneath them, with the thread under the needle, forming a loop. Pull through gently, then insert the needle a short way below, over the loop, forming a straight stitch which holds the loop securely. This last straight stitch can be made any length, or threaded with a bead, or made into a chain stitch. Fly stitch can be worked detached, vertically or horizontally. It can also be used as a couching stitch or on a raw edge.

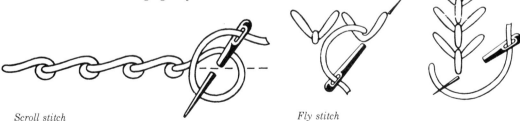

Scroll stitch

Fly stitch

Feather stitch: bring the needle through the fabric (A). Hold the thread down with the left thumb and insert the needle to the right on the same level; take a small stitch down, centrally, and pull the needle through, with the thread under it. Next, insert the needle a little to the left on the same level, and take another stitch down, centrally, keeping the thread under the needle. Do not pull tightly. This stitch is very decorative, and can be worked freely, as required.

Feather stitch

Closed feather stitch: work on two parallel lines, imagined or marked. Bring thread through on the left (A). Hold thread down with left thumb, insert needle at B and take a vertical stitch. Pull through, with the thread under the needle. Swing the thread over to the left, and with the thread under the needle, insert close to A and take a stitch vertically, bringing it out at D, keeping the thread under the needle and forming a series of triangular-shaped stitches. When practised, this is quite quick to work, and covers well, as the loops can be made fairly wide, if required. The triangles can be joined completely for quicker working.

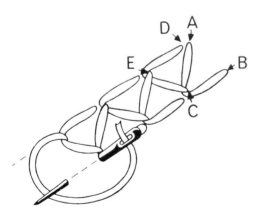

Closed feather stitch

Closed buttonhole stitch: bring needle through fabric (A), then insert higher up, to the right, and pull through at C, a short distance from A, with the thread under the needle. Insert needle again at B, but this time slant needle to the right, and bring it through on the lower line, with the thread under the needle. This stitch forms decorative triangles, which can be used on straight or circular shapes—the triangles can be varied in size.

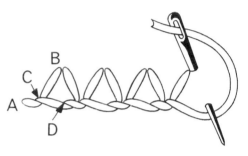

Closed buttonhole stitch

Twisted chain stitch: bring the needle through the fabric. Then, holding the thread down with the left thumb, insert needle to the left, over the thread, bringing it out a short distance away, through the loop of thread.

This is quicker to work than chain stitch, and can be varied by spacing and the positioning of the needle. It is a useful line stitch.

Twisted chain stitch

92

Open chain stitch: work on two parallel lines, imagined or marked. Bring needle through fabric (A), then holding thread down with left thumb, insert needle on the same level, a short distance away (B). Bring the needle through below where it emerged (C). Leaving the looped thread looser than usual, insert the needle on the opposite side (D), inside the looped thread. Bring it out on the opposite side, below and over the thread, to form the next stitch.

Once practised, this is an interesting stitch to use, especially good in surface embroidery for cellular effects. The spaces of the stitch can be varied easily, by making small or large loops.

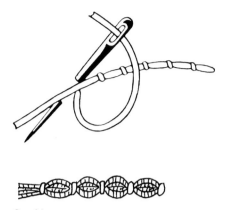

Couching

Roumanian couching: bring the needle through the fabric (A) and insert it where required, bringing it through with a small stitch. Take small stitches along the thread at intervals (B & C). The needle should then emerge ready for the next long thread. This is useful to fill an irregular space, using the same thread for both the couching and tying stitch.

Open chain stitch

Couching: lay a thread on the fabric, and fasten it down at intervals with a small stitch. The couched thread is usually thicker than the tying thread, and couching is therefore a useful method of attaching threads which are too thick to sew normally. The ends of thick threads can be pushed into the fabric with a knitting needle, crotchet hook or rug hook. If the thick thread is pulled loose between the tying threads it looks quite different. Other stitches can be used to tie down the thread—herringbone, cretan, open chain, closed feather, and so on. The tying thread can be matching or contrasting.

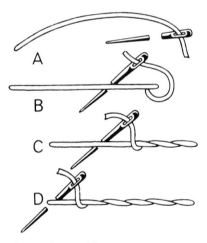

Roumanian couching

Laid work, with couching

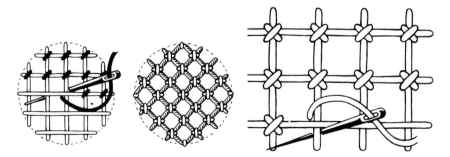

Laid work: long threads are laid or stitched across the space, horizontally and vertically. (Work in a frame for even tension.) They are then couched with a small stitch, where they cross. The spaces can be further decorated with cross stitches, beads, etc. Used extensively in Jacobean work.

Twisted insertion stitch: A decorative method of joining two pieces of fabric, braid, etc. If the fabrics are thin, they should be tacked on to paper the required distance apart before stitching. The insertion stitch (also known as faggotting) should not enter the paper. A small stitch is taken alternately on the top and bottom edges. The needle enters the edge from underneath, and is twisted round the thread before entering the opposite edge. This method can also be carried out with cretan stitch or herringbone (see 'Three Seasons', page 15).

TEXTURAL STITCHES
These are sometimes more complicated, but are well worth the extra effort to master them.

Double knot stitch: bring needle through fabric (A), then take a small stitch a short distance away (B). Pull needle through, then pass it under the stitch just formed, without piercing the fabric (C). With the thread under the needle, pass the needle under the stitch again, to the right (D). Gives a delightful beaded effect—use a thickish thread for a pronounced raised appearance.

French knots: bring the needle through the fabric, pull thread upwards with left thumb, then twist needle round it twice (A). Still holding the thread, insert needle close to where it emerged. Slide knot down as needle enters fabric, then bring needle out, ready to continue (B).

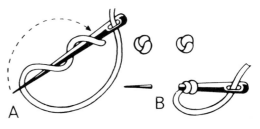

French knots

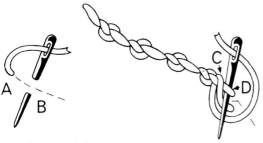

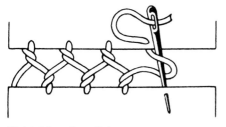

Twisted insertion stitch

Double knot stitch

Bullion stitch: bring needle through fabric, then insert it again, behind, taking a small back stitch, but do not pull needle right through. Twist thread round needle, as many times as required, and holding the left thumb on the coiled thread, pull needle through gently. Still keeping it in position, insert needle back where it emerged, and pull thread through.

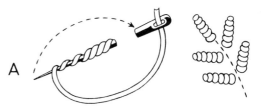

Bullion stitch

(left) '*Isle of Skye*', a 150cm square panel based on sketches of the island; the outer mount is divided into sections and joined with twisted insertion stitch (faggotting). By Eleri Mills

Knotted cable chain stitch: this is worked from right to left. Bring needle through fabric (A). Take a small stitch, a short distance away (B), inserting the needle at the back of the thread, and bringing it through with the thread under it. (This is a coral knot.) Pass the needle back, under the stitch just made, without piercing the fabric (C). Take a small stitch, close to the knot, with the thread under the needle (D). (NB: If the needle is placed closer to the knot than shown in the diagram near C, an interesting whorl is formed.)

Crested chain stitch: Practise with a medium woollen thread, working from right to left, on two imaginary parallel lines. Bring needle through on lower line, insert it on the upper line, to the left, through the looped thread (A). Pull needle through the chain stitch, then thread needle back through the straight sloping stitch (B). Insert needle on the lower line, where it first emerged, and bring it through, on the lower line, to the left of the chain above, and through the looped thread (C). Although this sounds complicated, it is quickly learned.

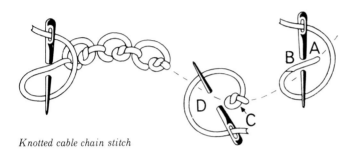

Knotted cable chain stitch

Vandyke stitch: bring needle through fabric (A), then take a small stitch above and to the right, horizontally (B). Insert the needle at C, and bring it through at D. Now, without piercing the fabric, pass the needle under the crossed threads, then insert again under C (E). Do not pull thread tightly. This is an unusual-looking stitch though it is difficult to achieve the angular appearance with some threads.

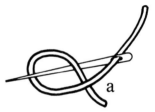

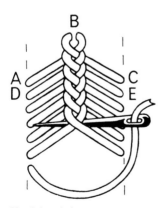

Vandyke stitch

Crested chain stitch

Open buttonhole filling: Bring the needle through at A, then take it up to B, and make a series of detached loops to fill the space.

Insert the needle at either end of the row, to secure the line of stitching (C). Bring it out below (D), then make loops into the row above, without entering the fabric. The last line of loops can be held down with a small stitch on the edge of the shape.

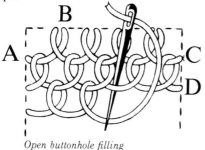

Open buttonhole filling

Knotted buttonhole filling: bring thread through fabric on the edge of a fold of fabric or marked shape, as at top left of drawing. Insert needle further along, and bring it through the loop of thread. Insert needle behind loop and bring through, over the thread, to form a small knot, shown in drawing. Pull through gently, to secure knot, then make next buttonhole stitch. As many rows as are needed can be worked, using the loops of the previous row, forming a detached filling which is very effective. Several stitches can be worked into one loop, experimentally. The last row can be anchored to the fabric with a small stitch in each loop. (See 'Green Rondels', page 79.)

Knotted buttonhole filling

Raised chain band: worked on a series of parallel straight stitches, placed fairly close together if using a thin thread, and wider if using a thicker one. The foundation stitches can be worked quite long if required, in which case it is advisable to stretch the fabric in a frame first.

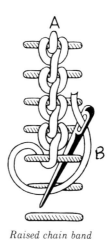

Raised chain band

Having worked the foundation, bring the needle through the fabric (A), then pass the needle upwards, under the first stitch, to the left. With the thread under the needle, pass the needle down under the stitch, to the right (B). Pull through gently—do not pull tightly. The needle does not penetrate the fabric while working the chain. This is not a difficult stitch to work, and it seems to enhance a design wherever used. It can be worked in different colours and threads.

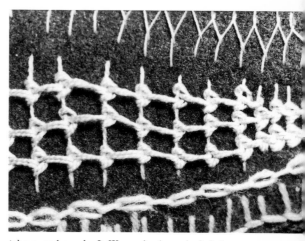

(above and overleaf) *Ways of using raised chain band*
Filling an irregular space—widely spaced, then more closely

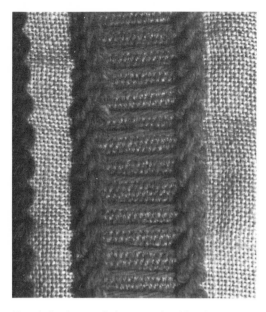

Foundation bars worked over a strip of hessian

One row of chain worked in rug wool, with polished oval wooden beads stitched in alternate spaces

Split, varnished bamboo has been applied with blanket stitch, with a row of raised chain band in a shiny crochet thread fixed on top. Two rows of chain are stitched between the bamboo pieces, in knitting wool (Kenneth Saunders)

Woven wheels (spiders' webs): wheels can be woven or back-stitched. If woven, they must have an odd number of 'spokes', but if they are backstitched, the number can be even or odd. For a woven wheel, make a fly stitch in a circle (marked or imagined) (A). Then add two more straight stitches, one on either side of the circle. Weave over and under the spokes, using matching or contrasting thread (B). The wheel can be filled, or left partly worked. Much larger wheels can be worked, using the same principle.

A backstitched wheel has an interesting ribbed appearance. Make the foundation spokes, then bring the needle up through the fabric, close to the centre, and push it under the spoke, backwards, bringing it up in front of the next spoke. Continue round, taking the needle backwards, then to the front of the next spoke. The needle should not enter the fabric.

The wheels can be worked small, as a filling, and combine well with beads, sequins, etc. A wide variety of threads can be used for the weaving.

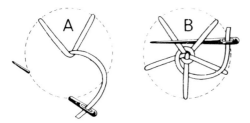

Woven wheels (spider's web)

Maltese tufts: best worked boldly, using a large-eyed needle and thick thread—three to six strands of wool, etc, depending on the scale. Insert needle into fabric from the *front* of the work, leaving the ends of the threads hanging, a little longer than the required tuft. Bring the needle through a short distance away, on the same level, to the left (b). Take the needle to the right and insert it (c), bringing it out close to (a) but on the left. Pull slightly, then trim both ends to make a tuft (d).

Velvet stitch: can be worked on fabric or canvas. Working from left to right, bring needle out at point marked by arrow, then insert at A. Bring needle out again at arrow, insert again at A, but this time leave the required length of thread, to form a loop. Bring needle out at B, level with arrow, holding loop down with left thumb if no gauge has been used. Insert needle at C and bring out at B—this will form a cross, holding the loop in place.

Repeat as required. Blocks of the stitch can be worked, the loops being either left as they are or cut. If the stitches are worked close together and the loops clipped short, it resembles the pile on carpet. Experiment with different thicknesses of thread. The loops can be worked over a card, knitting needle, dowel, etc; they can be made extra long to form a fringe (see Pulled Work, page 84).

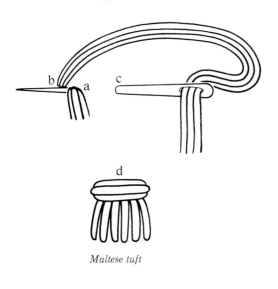

Maltese tuft

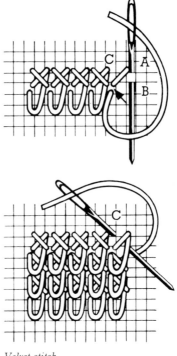

Velvet stitch

7 Textures

The tactile quality of a wall-hanging is usually an important element of its visual appeal. A design springs to life if texture is an integral part of it—it can be formed in a wide variety of ways, and should be chosen to suit the design.

Threads and Stitchery

These can create an infinite variety of textures. Literally any thread can be used, of any thickness, and stitches worked freely to build up textures. Thread can be knotted (a popular texture in eighteeenth-century embroideries), then couched over edges of fabric, or used as a filling or for linear effects.

Textured woollen threads are invaluable, as they can be used in so many different ways—couched down singly, or with several threads together; bunched or twisted; threaded through other stitches; combined with a thin silk thread, for some intriguing colour combinations. String, ribbons, tapes, braids, etc, can be looped, couched, woven or threaded, knotted, and so on, to create textures.

A rug fork can be used to make looped or fringed effects with a sewing machine. Use a large ball of thread if possible, and put it in a receptacle, on the floor as it unwinds. If using odd lengths, tie one piece to another, making sure that the knot is at the edge of the fork, so that it

Textures with fabric and thread: machine-quilted velvet, couched textured wool, raised chain band, raffine and plastic mesh (Kenneth Saunders)

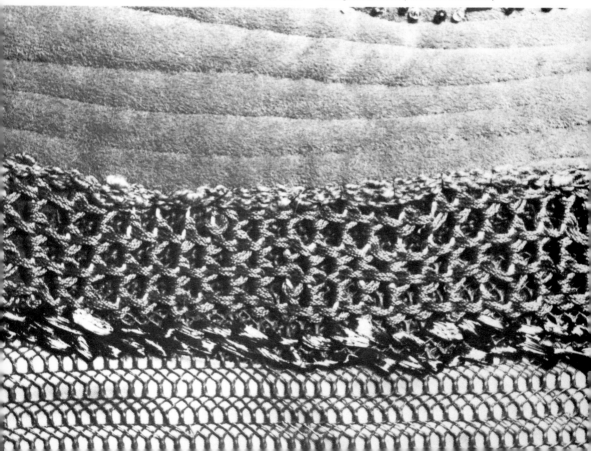

can be cut off after stitching. Wind the thread firmly and closely round the fork, up to the bend, and place into position on the fabric. The prongs of the fork should face the machine needle and pass either side of it—the work is machined centrally between the prongs, using a straight or zig-zag stitch (see drawing). It can be done with or without the sewing foot. When the bend of the fork is reached, leave the needle down in the

'Jamaica'. Copper and aluminium wire contrasted with fine silk threads, worked in various looped stitches, express the colours and atmosphere of a holiday in Jamaica. By Maria Fernandes (Terry Waddington)

work, and slide the fork away from the machine, releasing the loops. You can then wind more thread on to the fork and repeat the process.

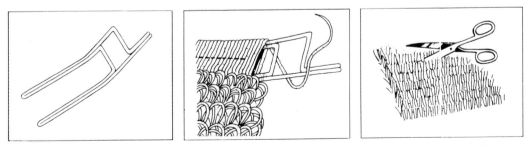

Looped or fringed effects made with a rug fork

Fabric Textures

Either the actual background fabric, or separate pieces applied to it can be tucked, ruched, gathered, pleated and so on. The reverse side of a fabric is often different from the right side. Experiments should be made—try withdrawing threads, or pushing them closer together. Holes can be made, and other fabrics can be placed behind them, or the holes can be neatened and used to suspend beads, etc.

Strips of fabric can be fringed, rolled, pleated or gathered, and stitched with a sewing machine in an irregular pattern, to make a rich texture. This looks effective with a limited colour range, with braids, ribbons, tapes, included.

Fabric strips can be threaded or hooked into canvas—the colours and textures can be built up to make an intriguing mixture (see 'Bodmin', page 104).

Use fabric and card together in a number of ways. Shapes of card can be covered with fabric and glued lightly on to the back of the card, then stitched into place on the background material. The card shape could be padded lightly, with foam or wadding; then, when it is covered with fabric, threads can be wound over it. The shapes are then applied to the background.

Long, thin strips of card can be covered with fabric, and stitched to the background by one edge only, leaving the other protruding from the background. (Cut fabric on the cross, if the card is to be curved.)

Other Textural Touches

Use beads, obtainable in a wonderful variety of shape and colour. Added with discretion, they can contribute textural interest in a number of ways. They should not be dotted around a design haphazardly, but placed to emphasise certain areas of it.

Sequins add sparkle and richness—use with moderation for impact. Other objects can be fixed to the background, whether covered with fabric, or held in place with stitchery. Pebbles, slices of wood, etc, can be covered with fabric, then stitched down. They can also be given an edging, perhaps of braid, for added texture.

Objects which cannot be pierced with a needle can be attached to the background by criss-crossing them with threads, thus partly obscuring the object, or slightly enclosed with stit-chery, round the edges. This is usually done with a buttonhole stitch. Work it close to the edge of the object, all round, on the background fabric; then work a second row, into the loops of the first, but pulling them tighter, to enclose the object and hold it in place.

Rings, cogs, washers, etc, are more easily attached, as they can be held in place with small straight stitches.

*

Personal Approach—Julia Caprara

Poetic Contrasts

The inspiration for my work can come from a poetic idea or theme; a visually inspiring texture or quality; a combination of fabrics and threads thrown together at random; or an evocative form or found object. My approach to stitchery is to set up for myself and the observer a series of problems in contrasts, and then resolve these contrasts into final harmony. The materials I use present contrasts—hessian and satin, mohair and sisal string, feathers and glass beads; qualities of shiny against matt, soft against hard, rough against smooth, cold against warm. Quilted and cut surfaces, torn edges and turned edges extend the contrasts.

Embroidery has such a wealth of techniques to work with that it is often difficult to know how to discipline methods into a valid expression. I try to evolve a series of stitch contrasts, clustering small stitch textures against more massive qualities, linear shapes against looped shapes. My favourite stitches are the families of straight stitches—darning, satin, buttonholes, cretan, fly stitches and isolated dot stitches, French knots, bullion knots, detached chain and seeding stitch. The freedom of expression is also extended by stitching areas of texture and applying these to other surfaces or textured grounds. This means that the heaviest and most massive wall-hanging can have the contrast of finely detailed embroidered sections to give contrast and variety.

Each piece of work develops from its own theme—'Love Tide', a circular panel on a macramé ring, was a series of unrelated forms of shell,

Julia Caprara's 'Galadriel's Mirror', a design based on the magic mirror of Queen Galadriel in J. M. Tolkien's Lord of the Rings. An inset mirror on a hardwood base is surrounded with textures of embroidery, pleated and crumpled fabrics and fringes in purple, blue and green

102

driftwood, stones and cork, integrated by stitchery techniques and fabric textures. Threads
and fabrics in greys, whites and browns were
used for tonal harmony, the aim being to achieve
richness and vitality through the weight and
variety of stitch textures, so that the light falling
across the surface would throw up a landscape of
hollow and rounded forms. 'St Swithun's Pavement' began in the chapel of St Swithun in
Winchester Cathedral, where the floor is paved
with glorious mellow medieval tiles in faded
pinks and oranges. Since the forms were fragmented, I began the fragmented patchwork of
the fabric pieces that build up the hanging. Again
a poem of contrasts, patterned opposed to plain
fabrics, the richness of velvet against the rawness
of leather and cotton, the shining surfaces of
handmade glass beads making a texture against
the soft flow of a fine wool fringe. The colour is
also an optical colour contrast of blue and orange
counterchange—blue embroidery texturing an

*'Bodmin'—rug canvas woven with fabric strips and
ribbons, with applied areas of weaving and tassels, in
purples, browns and blues to suggest the colours and
textures of Bodmin Moor in Cornwall. French knots
and fringes add to the textures. By Julia Caprara*

orange fabric, orange embroidery decorating
blue, to harmonise the total effect.

It is the fantasy of bitter-gentle contrasts, the
infinite variety of textures and colours, which
gives embroidery richness and poetry, making it
for me a totally expressive art form.

*

(right) *'Beachcomb'. Scrim, knitting, velvet and netting
are used here, with coiled string, pleated and ruched
braids and fabrics, beads and stitchery, to make an
irregular-shaped panel full of textures, providing both
visual and tactile interest*

104

INCORPORATING RELATED CRAFTS

A number of other crafts can be incorporated in a wall-hanging, to give a new and exciting dimension and texture. These include:

Macramé: particularly suited to some wall-hangings. It can be used to form part of the design itself; for edges or fringes; or for suspending the hanging. (Pieces of abandoned projects could be used with other collage items!)

Knitting: unusual knitted shapes and textures are effective on a hanging, using threads (not necessarily wool) thick, thin, matt or shiny, depending on the effect required. Unravelled pieces from old jumpers, etc, could also be used. Different-sized needles will produce fine close work, or an open lace-like effect.

Weaving: closely allied to some forms of stitchery, it can form an integral part of a hanging. It can be worked into a fabric, or on threads laid on the surface of the fabric. It can also be worked separately, then applied to the background. A wide variety of threads can be used, including unusual types such as tape, bandage, ribbons, etc (see 'Sun', page 39).

Crochet: this can be worked in a wide variety of patterns and textures, using different threads and hooks. Long lines of chain can be couched, or used to outline shapes. Pieces can be worked separately, then applied.

Lace-making: this craft has enjoyed a revival in recent years, and lace itself, or lace-making techniques, adapt well to wall-hangings. The scale can be varied to suit the design—work with fine thread for delicate effects, thicker threads for a bold approach. A freer approach to colour would add a new dimension.

Rug-making: the techniques used in making rugs can provide exciting textural effects for hangings. Experiments should be made to determine the best method and thread for a specific part of a design (see 'Bodmin', page 104).

Narrow strips of knitted garter stitch in textured and plain wools are woven and pleated to form tunnels (Knitting Craft Group)

Crocheted split circles, with two or more stitches worked into each chain to produce a buckled effect. Small bobbles provide contrast and binca canvas gives an unusual background (Knitting Craft Group)

Interlaced strips of knitting suggest growth of plants or trees. The curves are made by knitting incomplete rows, then turning. Openings are made by the method used for making buttonholes (Knitting Craft Group)

8 Cords, Tassels and Fringes

Haberdashery departments sell a wide range of cords, braids, fringes and so on, but if the correct type and colour cannot be found they can be made by hand—often more satisfactorily, too, as they can be matched to the hanging, using threads already in it, which gives a unified finish to the work.

CORDS

Simple twisted cord: experiment to find out how many strands of thread look right, and the length required. Take two strands, each half the thickness you want the finished cord and three times the required finished length. Knot them together at either end and fix one end to a board or other surface with a drawing pin. Twist the other end round and round (use a pencil) until it is tightly twisted. Fold it in the centre, take out the drawing pin, and let the end go. It will twist together into a cord—smooth out any wrinkles. For a thicker cord, use more strands.

Plaited cord: looks effective in wool, and can be made to any thickness. Cut a suitable number of threads, divisible by three, to make the correct thickness, and knot them together at the top (a).

Secure them with a drawing pin to a board, and intertwine the three sections, regularly, to make a plait (b).

The ends can be trimmed and finished decoratively (c).

TASSELS

Basic tassel: cut a piece of stiff card the length of the required tassel, then wind thread round to the thickness required (a). Cut the threads free, at one edge, then stitch or bind them all together in the centre, using the same thread, double. The ends can be left in the centre (b).

The tassel can be given a 'head' by binding a

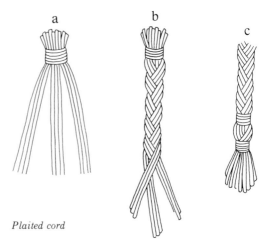

Plaited cord

short distance down, with a matching or contrasting cord. Beads, etc, can be threaded immediately above it. The top portion can be tightly bound with matching or contrasting thread. A ring (covered with thread or left plain) can be tied into the tassel (c–f).

Felt tassel: cut felt into a long narrow strip, the size and length required. With sharp scissors, make a series of cuts, along the length, close together, but leaving a margin at one end, uncut. Roll the felt round tightly, and bind or stitch the top. These felt tassels usually suit larger hangings best, especially if suspended by a cord or thick thread. The cord could be threaded with beads.

POMPOMS

Cut two identical circles of card, the size required, and remove a small circle from the centre. Wind thread round the card, taking the thread through the centre hole. If a small pompom is being made, thread it with a needle, using a thick or double thread (a). Cover the card quite thickly, then

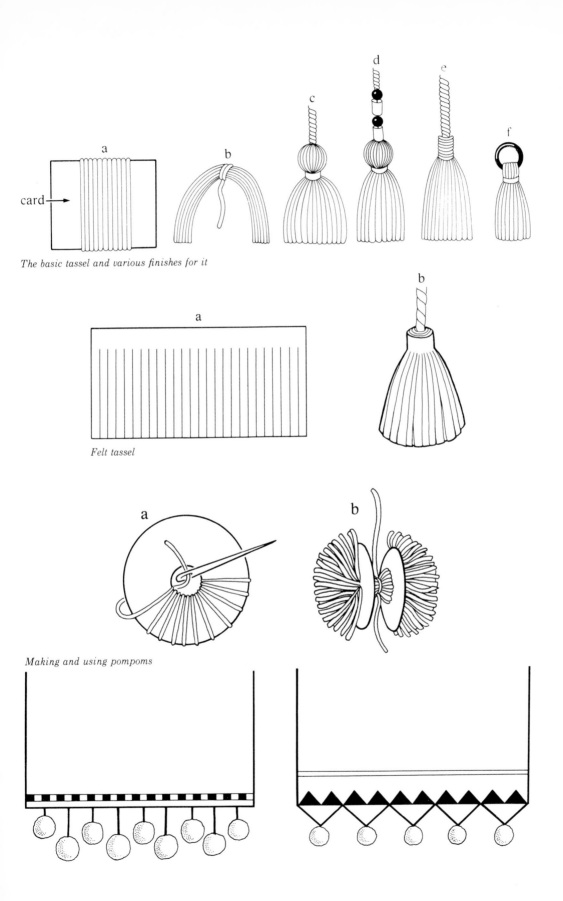

The basic tassel and various finishes for it

Felt tassel

Making and using pompoms

carefully snip the thread free round the edge of the card (b). Do not pull the card right out until the threads have been secured in the centre, with a matching thread, used double. Tie very tightly, then ease off the card.

The centre thread used for tying can also be used for stitching to the hanging. Fluff out the pompom, and trim if necessary.

These can be made in different colours, or multi-coloured, using the same threads as in the hanging; they can be incorporated into the work or used to make an edging, on threads of different lengths.

FRINGES AND EDGINGS

Hemstitched fringe: worked on a single fabric. Pull out some threads, on the lower edge, horizontally, leaving the rest to be removed later. Hemstitch at the top of the fringe, with a matching or contrasting thread, taking three or four threads in the needle each time. Remove the remaining threads, and trim the fringe if necessary.

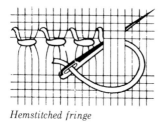

Hemstitched fringe

Basic knotted fringe: a wide variety of threads can be used to match the hanging—wool, cotton, silks, tubular rayon, string, etc. Wind a long length of thread over a piece of card cut to the required length, allowing a little extra for the knotting-in (a). Cut the threads along one edge only. Thread each length, doubled, into a large-eyed needle (b).

Stretch out the lower edge of the hanging, fixing it with pins to a board, to keep it still. Working on the right side, push the needle through to the wrong side of the hem, close to the edge. Pull the needle halfway through, then remove it, and push the two ends of the thread through the loop; then pull close to the hem. Continue along the hem, placing the lengths close together (c, d, e).

Variations can be introduced in the fringe by using macramé knotting techniques, or suspend-

ing other items from it—rings, beads, etc. Very long fringes can be incorporated into the design of the hanging, or a small hanging can be given more emphasis with a long fringe.

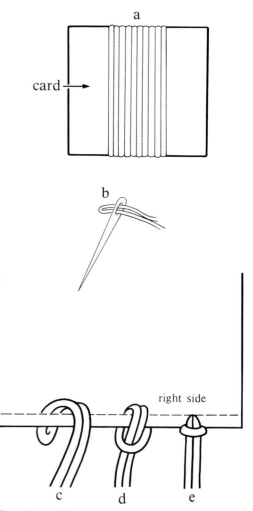

Basic knotted fringe

Looped edging: various looped edgings can be made. Several threads can be threaded in the needle together, and one of the loop stitches can be used. If the thread is thick, such as tubular rayon or rug wool, it can be pinned in loops along the hem, then stitched into place on the back of the hanging. The loops could be all the same size or could be of uneven lengths, or staggered, working more than one layer. A matching braid could be stitched along the hem to balance and unify it.

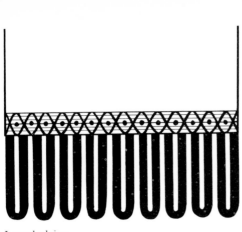

Looped edging

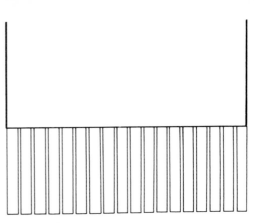

Ribbon edging

Ribbon edging: this could be one colour, or multi-coloured, to suit the design. Decide on the length required, allowing extra to attach to the back of the hanging. Ribbon could be looped, or cut with a pointed edge. Tack it to the hanging, then when spacing is correct stitch it into place.

Quill edging: this is made from squares of folded fabric, making an unusual finish which would be particularly suitable for a patchwork or appliqué hanging. Each 'quill' is cut from a square of fabric, three times the finished width; eg a square of 9cm will give a finished quill of 3cm.

Cut squares required, then fold in half, and press down fold (a). Fold over each side to make a triangular shape (b). Fold over each side again, one-third along (c and d). Pin or tack along the straight edge to hold the quill together, then pin into place along the hem, on the back of the hanging. Stitch into place (e).

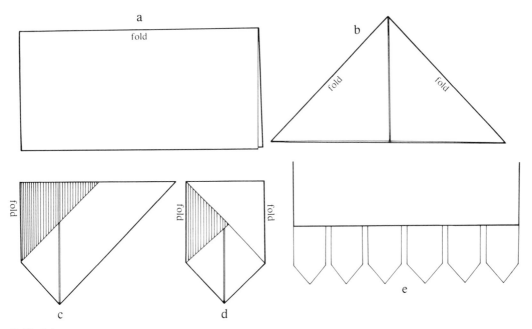

Quill edging

Triangular edging: each triangle is made from a square of fabric. The finished long edge is the same measurement as the cut squares—if 8cm squares are cut, the long edge to attach to the hanging will be 8cm. This makes it easy to calculate the number required.

Fold each square diagonally (a and b), then once again, to form a triangle (c). Press. Tack them to the wrong side of the hanging, making sure that the open side of every triangle is placed in the same direction. Stitch firmly into place (d). Another layer could be added behind or on top, using a combination of the colours in the hanging (e).

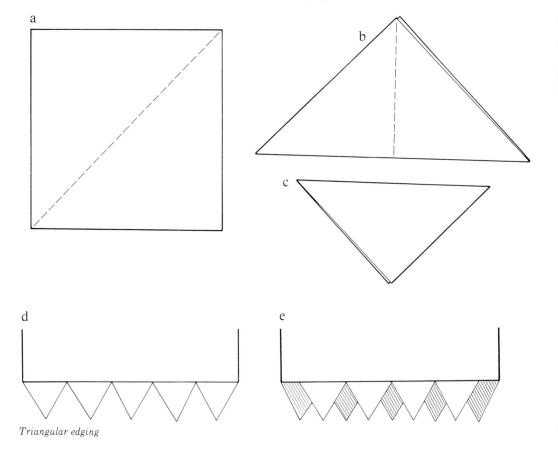

Triangular edging

114

9 Making-up

SOFT HANGINGS

Loose, pliable-looking hangings have an indefinable quality, particularly suited to some types of design and situation. They have always been popular for ecclesiastical work, often being displayed as banners. Due to the absence of a rigid mounting board, they may be a little more difficult to hang satisfactorily, but are well worth the effort.

Large hangings which are to be hung some distance away from the viewer can be given bold treatment with simple shapes, stitchery and braids, etc. On the other hand, quite small hangings can be arresting, if the design is interesting.

Soft hangings can be made from a wide variety of fabrics, and methods. If they are lined, the material can be the same as the hanging, but generally a thinner fabric is used. Interlining can be used to give extra weight and body. The top and bottom edges can be finished in a number of different ways—sometimes identically, but often in two different yet complementary ways. Soft hangings give scope for interesting treatments on the outer edges.

As methods of hanging influence the finishing of the top edge, it should be decided in advance which to use. Wooden dowel rods can vary in thickness from very fine to broom-handle width. Split dowel is useful, as it has a flat side, which is preferable for some hangings. Metal tubing can be bought from DIY shops or hardware departments, and cut to the length required. Bamboo, too, is obtainable in different thicknesses, and can be used split if required. Wooden or metal rings can be acquired from a variety of sources, including macramé suppliers, who have an interesting range of rods and other fitments.

Soft hangings can be made up in three basic ways:

with a single layer of fabric
with a lining
with three layers—top fabric, interlining and lining.

Single-layer Hangings

A wide variety of fabrics can be used to make a single-layer hanging, from coarse hessian and furnishing fabrics to fine woollens and linen. They are effective in all types of scrim. If they are made in a loosely woven fabric, or have open spaces as part of the design, they may allow the colour of the wall behind to show through, which should be taken into account.

When stitching, try to finish off the back of the work neatly, weaving in loose ends, to make them secure. (If silky threads have been used, which show signs of working loose, try brushing over them with Marvin Medium. It will dry transparent and secure the threads.)

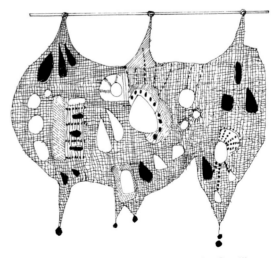

Soft hanging in loose-woven fabric (drawn by Camilla Nock)

The sides of the fabric can be finished in various ways—a hem can be turned, and slip-stitched on the back. If the material is thick, or frays, a binding or facing tape could be used, either as a decorative feature, or turned to the back of the hanging, and slip-stitched or herring-boned into place. Braid or cord could make a decorative finish on the right side of the work.

It is not essential to mitre a corner, but if you wish to, mark the actual fold line of the turnings by creasing, then cut off a diagonal piece of fabric allowing enough to turn over on the corner (a). Turn over the diagonal cut edge, so that the fold of it just rests on the marked corner (b). Press down firmly, then fold over each side, on the marked fold line, and tack down on the wrong side, turning a narrow hem (c). Slipstitch into position (d).

If mitring for the first time, practise with folded paper first, to ascertain the diagonal cut and fold. If this is cut incorrectly, the material may be spoilt.

A single-layer hanging often looks best with a simple rod suspension, threaded through a channel made by turning over the top of the fabric, stitched by hand or machine (a). If the stitching shows, it could be covered with braid, etc, or couching. An interesting drawn-thread border could be worked, if the fabric and design is

suitable, which could fasten down the top edge, and give a decorative finish at the same time, (b).

If a cord suspension is preferred, the hanging may need a wooden strip, attached at the back, to prevent sagging. Cut a flat strip of wood, slightly smaller than the width of the hanging, and attach it to the back, over the folded hem, with large oversewing stitches and strong thread (c). The cord can then be stitched to the hanging, or to the wooden strip. Or the wooden strip could be covered with fabric, then stitched to the hanging.

The lower edge can be fitted with a wooden rod, to match the top, which will also weight it down. Alternatively, it could be given a hem-stitched self-fringe, a hand-made or a ready-made fringe.

Lined Soft Hangings
A lining will protect the back from dust, conceal all the worked threads, and give a neat finish to it. It can be made from the same fabric as the hanging itself, or a thinner one, such as curtain lining, or calico. It is advisable to pre-shrink thinner linings before use. Decide which method will be used to finish the top and bottom edges (see suggestions on next pages).

Deal with the sides first—tack a single turning (approx 3cm) on the hanging, on the wrong side. Cut the lining to cover the hanging, allowing 2cm extra for turnings.

Tack the 2cm turning allowance to the wrong side on the lining fabric (sides only). Mark the centres of both fabrics, top and bottom; match them (wrong sides together), pin and tack them together. The lining should be narrower than the hanging, so make any necessary adjustments.

Slip-stitch the sides together, catching the lining edges, to the tacked turning of the hanging, making sure the stitches do not penetrate the front of the hanging. Press lightly on the wrong side only of the hanging.

The top and bottom edges of the lining are stitched into position when the hanging itself is completed, with tabs, fringes, etc, so that it

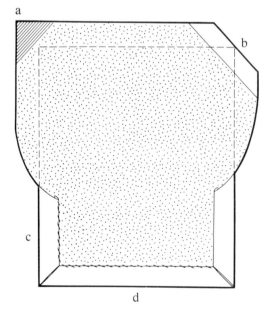

c

d

Mitring a corner

'Orbed in a Rainbow, Throned in Celestial Sheen'. Using paper stencils, fabric dyes have been sprayed on to cotton gaberdine to form the background for this carefully worked-out design. Machine embroidery (whip stitch) has been applied. The card mount has been painted with gouache and acrylics, with an added arch of wrapped threads. By Verina Warren

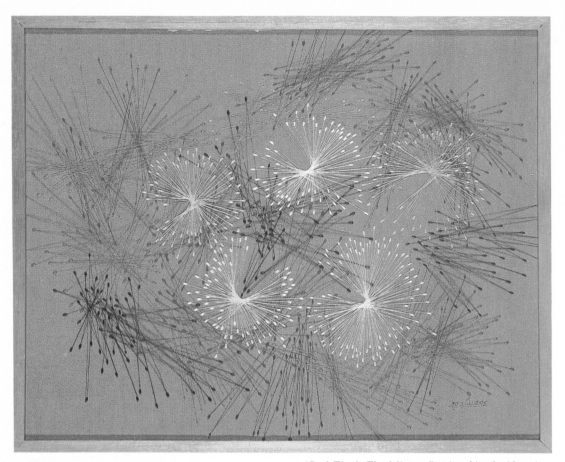

'Seed Time'. The delicate effect is achieved with satin-stitch beads made in free machine embroidery. The long connecting threads must be stretched on a rigid board to keep the tension, so this kind of design can only be used on a panel. For directions on how to make this, see Project 17 at the back of the book. By Joy Clucas (English Sewing Ltd)

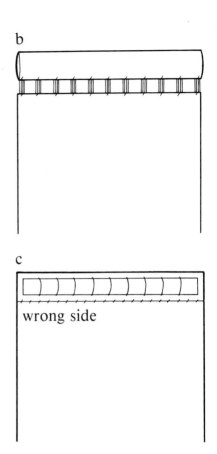

Suspension methods for a single-layer hanging

covers any untidy edges. Pin and tack the lining to the top and bottom edges, turning in the raw edges. Slip-stitch into position.

Leave the finishing of the lower edge of the hanging for a few days—this allows the fabrics to settle, and any final adjustments can be made.

On a large soft hanging, it may be necessary to attach the lining in the centre, vertically from top to bottom. This should be done after stitching the first side. Use a loose herringbone or blanket stitch, spacing the stitches out, with the lining folded back. The stitches should take up only a tiny amount of fabric on the back of the hanging, so that they are invisible from the front.

The top of the hanging can be finished in a number of different ways to suit the hanging. Some basic finishes are:

Concealed wooden strip: cut a flat wooden strip 1cm shorter than the width of the top edge. Place it in position on top of the lining, and fold the hanging fabric and lining together over the wooden strip, tucking the raw edges under it. Catch-stitch this folded hem to the lining, stitching up the side openings as well.

A cord or hanging rings can then be stitched to the rigid top edge, wherever required.

Channel and rod: the lining should extend most of the length of the hanging, stopping short by approximately 2cm. Turn this allowance over, tack down, then turn over a larger amount to accommodate the rod easily but not too loosely. Tack, then slip-stitch firmly to the lining (a).

Alternatively, an extra piece of facing fabric could be stitched to the turned-over hem, to take the rod (b).

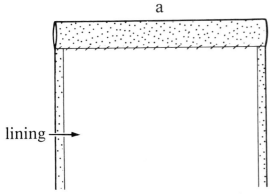

a

lining

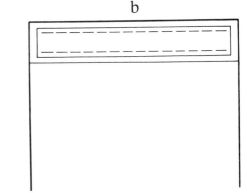

b

Channel and rod suspension for a lined hanging

Concealed rings and rod: this method can be used with any hanging which has a straight top. Stitch curtain rings to the turned-over hem, at the top of the hanging, placing them a few centimetres below the top edge. The rings should be stitched to stand away from the hanging. Through the rings insert a rod slightly shorter than the width of the hanging.

Fabric tabs and rod: decide on the number of tabs required—wide ones can be spaced further apart than narrow ones. They should be cut long enough to fold over the rod, and extend 3–6cm beyond it (depending on the weight of the rod) into the hanging. They are cut twice the finished width, plus 1cm seam allowance, from matching or contrasting fabric. (Check one to ensure you have the correct size.)

Machine the long sides, wrong sides together, 1cm from edge (a). Turn to right side, with seam line in centre back of tab, and press lightly (b).

Fold in half, pin them into position on the hanging. Check that enough space has been left for the rod to pass through them, then stitch firmly into place (c).

If using on a single-fabric hanging, neaten the ends of the tabs. If using on a lined hanging, fit the lining over the ends of the tabs to conceal them (d).

'Spring Green', a soft hanging interlined with cotton duck. Circles—curtain-rings, washers, lampshade rings—have been buttonholed with green crochet thread, filled with needleweaving, then applied to a pale green textured furnishing fabric which has been lightly machine quilted. Pale green and orange beads have been added and a tubular rayon macramé thread has been couched on either side. The edge is finished with small buttonholed curtain-rings and a tubular rayon fringe

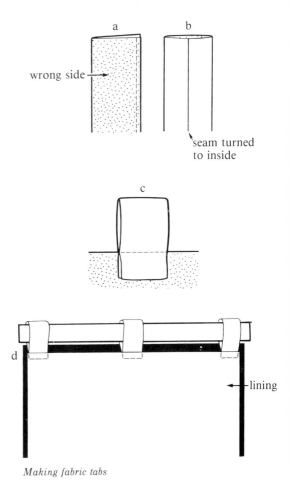

Making fabric tabs

121

Hanging with Velcro: if a batten is fixed to the wall (slightly narrower than the hanging) the hanging can be fitted with Velcro. Even large hangings will be secure, so it could be used for a hanging which is intended to be left permanently in one place. Stitch the softer strip to the top edge of the back of the hanging, very firmly. Fix the other strip to the batten, with small tacks. Press the hanging into place.

Shaped edge: a shaped edge creates interest and looks unusual—it may be scalloped, triangular or irregular to suit the design.

Cut a paper pattern first, to check that it will fit properly, then mark the shapes on the back of the work. If making curves, use a saucer for a guide. Remember to snip curved edges for stitching (a). Cut out the shapes, allowing a turning of 1cm. Tack the turnings to the wrong side of the work. Cut a lining to match, tack the turnings, then slip-stitch the two together, with the lining fabric just below the edge of the hanging so that it does not show on the right side. (If a shaped edge is cut on a single hanging, the edges could be bound with a bias strip, or neatened with a facing.)

The cut shapes could take a rod: turn them and stitch a channel in each one (b).

Finishing the lower edge: the lower edge of a hanging can be finished in a number of different ways. It can be identical to the top—eg be given tabs and rod—or be given a fringe, tassels and so on. If the work is very large and heavy, the lower edge should be left 'open', to avoid pulling. Whatever is decided, it should have some relation to the rest of the hanging and be in keeping with the design. There are a number of suggestions in Chapter 8 and in the photographs.

Hangings with Interlining

Interlining can be thick calico, cotton duck, sailcloth, Vilene, tailor's canvas, blanket, etc. Cut it to the size required for the finished hanging, with any special shaping included. Calico and cotton duck should be pre-shrunk, by damping well, then ironing dry, before use.

Place the hanging face-down on a clean surface. Mark centre points at top and bottom of the hanging and the interlining.

Place the interlining centrally on the wrong side of the hanging, matching centre markings, with a margin of the hanging fabric projecting clear all round it.

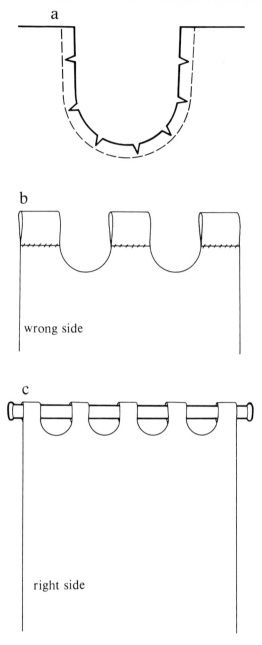

Making a shaped edge

(right) *The distinctive shaped top of this banner has been outlined with Russian braid, emphasising the 'spire' design* (Wippell Mowbray Ltd)

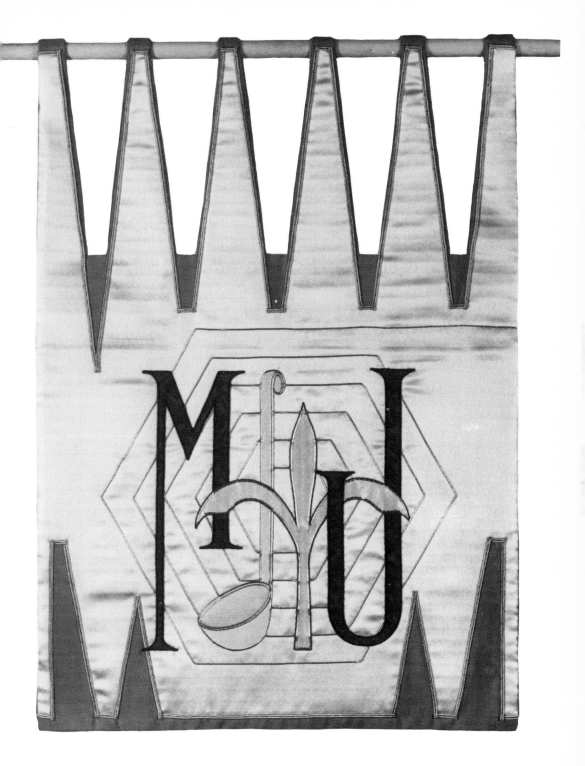

Turn the sides of the fabric on to the interlining. Tack, then slip-stitch or herringbone into place. Turn over the top and bottom edges similarly, leaving the sides open if required to take a rod, etc. Alternatively finish with a shaped edge, as previously described.

Cut a lining material to cover the back of the hanging, allowing turnings of 1cm. Tack and press them, then slip-stitch into place, covering the interlining and turned edges of the hanging.

PANELS

Panels can be made up in a wide variety of different ways, and give greater scope than other types of wall-hangings for original mounting. They can vary in shape enormously—they may be long and narrow, square, rectangular, oblong or irregular for instance. They may be simply mounted, or employ several different framing techniques. Suspension can take a number of different forms—by a cord (which may or may not be visible), or with rings, tabs, a rod and so on.

Directions are given for the basic mounting methods, and also some variations. When some of these are tried out, other ideas will occur, to suit individual requirements. By tackling the mounting oneself, ideas can be worked out, and changes made as required. It is a very rewarding task, as each panel can be given a different treatment, and the finished work looks immeasurably improved when stretched on a rigid board.

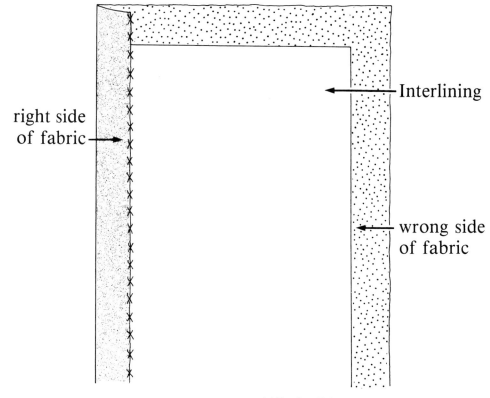

right side of fabric

Interlining

wrong side of fabric

Adding interlining

(right) Panels made up of small units; see also Project 15, page 169

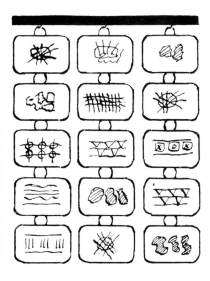

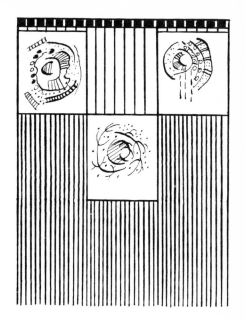

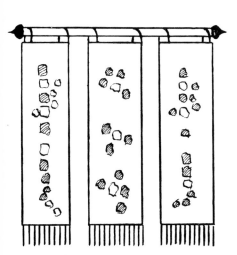

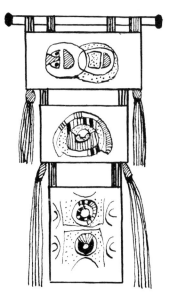

*Simple, basic mounting on hardboard: 'Pine Cone'
consists of quill patchwork in a variety of sizes and
fabric textures, in tones of one colour which give
subtlety to the design. The centre is filled with beads
and French knots. By Jane Blair* (Charles Risk)

Mounting Boards

A number of different boards are available for mounting and it is well worth spending time selecting them. Your local DIY shop should be able to advise you—a helpful assistant is an asset. Off-cuts, often just the right size for panels, are sometimes available at a reduced price. Board can also be cut to unusual shapes, if you explain what you want and provide measurements or a paper pattern.

Hardboard: a popular board for panels, and reasonably priced. It is available in thin, medium and heavy-duty thickness, and varies in colour from pale fawn to dark brown. It can also be used as a visible mount, where the colour can be chosen to complement the design—varnish can be applied, preferably several coats.

Thin hardboard is used mainly for mounting small panels, backing work of all sizes, and some window mounts.

Medium hardboard is the most useful for mounting the majority of panels—it is sturdy enough to take the strain of the taut fabric, unless the panel is very large. It can be cut quite successfully with a good craft knife.

Heavy-duty hardboard can be used for large panels, as it is stronger, but it is also heavier. If this could be a problem, consider some of the other, lighter boards. All hardboards may warp slightly—wooden battens could be added on the back if required.

Boards of varying thicknesses: a wide range of different types of board used for domestic purposes are suitable as mounts.

Plywood is made in a variety of thicknesses—from paper-thin to a thick rigid board which is unlikely to warp.

Chipboard is also available in different thicknesses, but is inclined to be heavy.

Blockboard is made up of layers of wood, and will take screws in the back.

There are a number of *lightweight boards* used for insulation, ceilings, etc. They are easily cut with a sharp knife, so are particularly suitable for shaped boards. They are inclined to warp, so this factor should be taken into consideration for large panels; battening could be fixed to overcome the problem.

Window Mounts

A 'window' of any shape can be cut from a suitable material and placed over the panel, allowing the work to show through. A wide range of materials can be used, including cork tiles, card, balsa wood, thin hardboard, plywood, leather and leatherette, felt, baize, oiled manilla paper, and specially prepared coloured mounting card (sold for picture framing).

Frames

A very good range of mouldings can be bought for a frame, from simple plain wood to ornately gilded creations. If carefully matched to the panel, it will noticeably enhance it. Most people do not wish to make up their own frame, preferring to have it made professionally, but in fact you can do it yourself, with practice, using a simple mitre box, clamps and saw. This would save expense, in the long run, if frames were required regularly.

When ordering a frame, include the hardboard cut to fit loosely, at the same time, if mounting on it. It is preferable to do this rather than to mount the work first and then order the frame separately afterwards: if the frame comes fractionally small, you will have to reduce the mounted work to fit.

There is also a good selection of ready-made frames available from shops and stores. Packs of pre-cut lengths which are slotted together to make a frame of the required dimension are also sold, including metal ones. Aluminium framing is rather expensive but suits some modern work.

Old frames can be acquired from auction sales, secondhand shops and market stalls. Check that the corners are in good condition. Wooden frames, begrimed with age, often clean up very well (see later).

Wooden oval and circular frames are very attractive, but rather more difficult to obtain. Picture-framers may have some in stock, or will get them to order. If there is a local craftsman specialising in wood-turning, he may be able to provide a turned circular frame to a specific size. There are some oval-shaped metal frames available, made for photographs, which could be used for small work.

Unusual frames can be made from other materials. Bamboo can be obtained in different thicknesses—it varnishes or stains easily, and can be split, if required. Basketry cane can be coiled into a circular 'frame', twisting several strands together. Wire lampshade rings can be bought in a wide range of sizes—they can be fixed together in various ways, or squashed into irregular shapes if required. Plastic tubing may suit some experimental work—it can be formed into unusual shapes, and there are a number of thicknesses.

Polyurethane varnishes can be obtained in clear, matt, semi-gloss or high gloss finish. For most purposes, semi-gloss is recommended. Stain varnish, eg light oak, dark oak, etc, is useful for refurbishing a frame, and for changing the colour of dowel rods, bamboo, etc.

When applying varnish, ensure that the surface is clean, then rub with a fine sandpaper for best results. Always apply the varnish thinly and evenly. Several coats, sanded between layers, are better than one thick layer.

Restoring old wooden frames: old frames are often attractive when cleaned, revealing interesting wood-grain patterns. Remove the backing and glass carefully. If the back of the frame has brown paper stuck to it, remove this: damp it with an old cloth to loosen it. Clean the frame, rubbing gently with a fine steel wool and white spirit. Follow the grain of the wood while rubbing. If there is a thick coat of varnish, it may be necessary to remove it with paint stripper.

When the frame is clean and dry, it can be wax-polished or varnished. If it is badly stained, it could be painted with gloss paint.

Damaged frames can be covered with fabric, using the same method as for a partly glued window mount (adding a thin foam padding or other interlining, if necessary), or bound with thread. This is particularly suitable for needle-weaving, etc, or when incorporating scrims and hessian.

Other Mounting Requirements

Craft knife—Stanley or similar, for cutting board and card
Scissors—separate pairs for paper and fabrics
Hessian binding—for neatening the back of some panels (made of jute, natural colour)
Masking tape—for neatening the back, with a rigid frame
Brads—small headless nails
Small-headed hammer
Fine short tacks
Nylon hanging cord
Picture hooks and screw eyes
Ruler
Adhesives

Basic Mounting for Panels

Use for rectangular, square or oblong shapes.

Obtain medium hardboard cut to the required shape and size. (Thin hardboard, or strong card can be used if the panel is small.) If your stitched fabric is thin, the board should be covered with a thin lining fabric—sheeting, calico, etc. Glue this lightly to the board, cutting it the same size as the board.

Mark the centre of the board, at top and sides, then mark the centres of the stitched panel. Place the board on the wrong side of the hanging, centres matched, with the inner lining (if used) next to it (a).

Dealing with the shortest sides first, glue them to the back of the board, using Copydex or a similar fabric adhesive, avoiding the actual edge of the board. Pull the second side taut, and re-do the first if necessary.

There is a fold of fabric at each corner—cut away a small rectangle (b). A mitred corner is not recommended, as the tension on the fabric is better achieved without a cornerwise removal of fabric. Glue the other sides firmly on to the board, checking constantly that work does not show wrinkles and is correctly aligned (c). Re-glue any side which has not been pulled tightly enough.

Neatening the backing: there are two methods of doing this. Either completely cover it with a matching fabric—this is most suitable for small panels—or use a wide hessian binding. This is a new method which is useful on larger panels.

To cover the back completely, cut a matching or contrasting fabric 2cm larger than the mounted work, and tack this turning to the wrong side of the fabric. Pin it into position on the back of the mounted panel, covering all raw edges. Using strong matching thread, slip-stitch the fabric to the panel. Stitch two curtain rings at either side, and thread with nylon cord.

For the second method, obtain hessian binding, as used in upholstery and for carpets (approx 6cm wide). Cut four lengths—two to go right across the top and bottom of the panel, and two for the sides, to fit under the edge of the top and bottom pieces (first drawing).

The outer edges are stitched first, with strong buttonhole thread, used double. Place the top piece on the back of the top edge, a short distance from it. Stitch firmly together as in second drawing. Repeat with the other pieces, placing

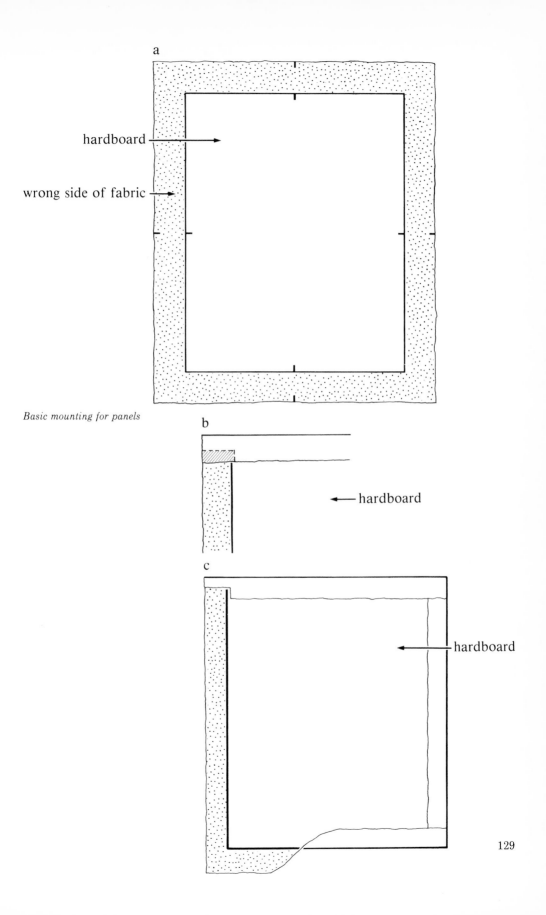

a

hardboard

wrong side of fabric

Basic mounting for panels

b

hardboard

c

hardboard

129

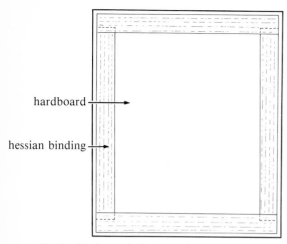

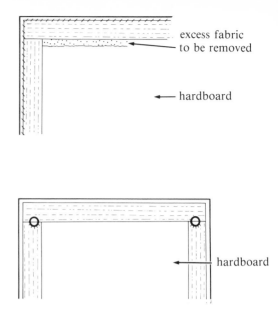

excess fabric
to be removed

← hardboard

← hardboard

Hessian binding method of mounting

the two sides (cut edges) under the top and bottom pieces. Buttonhole the raw edges of the top and bottom pieces. Then trim away any surplus material, so that it all lies neatly under the binding. Stitch two curtain rings to the binding, where the inner corners meet, as in third drawing.

Now glue down the inner edges of the binding to the hardboard, using a contact adhesive, eg Evostick, and enclosing all the raw edges. (Check the adhesive, to ensure it does not come through, if you are not using hessian.)

Attach a thin nylon hanging cord, using it double, threading through the curtain rings. The cord should not be visible on the right side.

Laced mounting: instead of glueing, the fabric can be laced tightly across the back of a board. This is most suitable for small panels, but not if the material is flimsy or loosely woven.

Centre the fabric on the board, which should be slightly thicker than hardboard, to take pins in the side. Begin by pinning in the centres of all four sides, pulling the fabric smoothly over the board, working from the right side, with the work face upwards. Push more pins in each side, adjusting any which need it, until the fabric is taut and even.

Fold over the spare fabric to the back of the board, and using a long, strong thread (double if necessary) begin lacing from one side to the opposite side, pulling the thread tightly. Fasten

off the end securely, and continue until all the sides are laced, pulling the thread tightly all the time to pull the fabric taut.

Neaten the backing by covering it with fabric, as described above.

A simplified form of this method is also possible, using thinner board, eg hardboard, and no pins, adjusting and pulling the fabric as necessary.

Mounting Variations

Double fabric mount: many panels are improved by double mounting, which forms a matching or contrasting surround, focusing attention on the mounted design and enhancing it.

Having mounted the panel itself, as in basic mounting described earlier, obtain a second piece of medium hardboard, cut larger than the basic panel, allowing whatever margin is required. Cover it with fabric, as in basic mounting, but the interlining may be omitted.

Place the stitched panel on the outer mount, with centres matched, or however it is required. Secure the corners temporarily, with a pin. Stitch each corner securely with strong matching thread. This may be sufficient if the panel is small. It can be stitched into position all the way round if necessary (a curved needle may be helpful).

Neaten the back with either of the methods suggested.

130

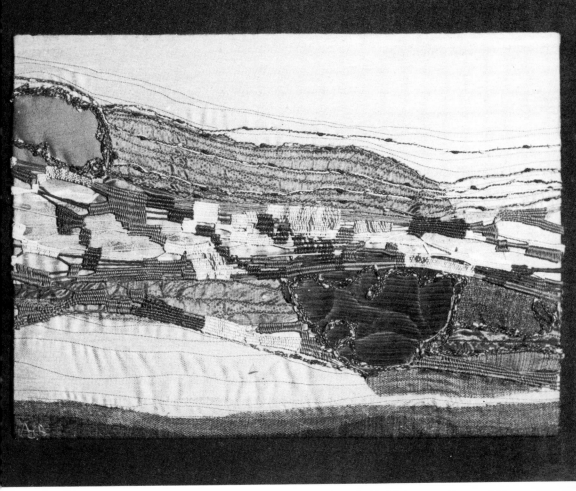

'Estuary'. A double fabric mount. Green and blue
applied fabrics, with padded corduroy, couched threads
and needleweaving

Double fabric mounting

Mounting on battening: wooden battens can be cut from soft wood, approximately 5mm × 25mm ($\frac{1}{4}$ × 1in), and fixed together with small panel pins. The wood need not be mitred, as it will not be seen. Stretch the work over the battening, and fix with drawing-pins first. Then remove the pins, one by one, replacing with a staple or small panel pin. If the back requires neatening, tack hardboard or card into position (first covering with matching fabric, if required).

Using masking tape, or strong sticky-backed paper, stick it partly over the frame, and partly on to the card, to cover the edges on all sides.

Screw eyes should be fixed into the frame, and threaded with nylon hanging cord. Make sure the cord does not show on the right side when hung. The eyes are obtainable in different sizes—suit the size and weight of your panel.

Builder's moulding: wooden mouldings used in the building trade for doors, windows, etc, can be made into frames, and are reasonably priced. They do not have a recess for fitting the panel, but this can be rectified by fixing a simple wooden strip underneath (a). It need not be mitred, as it is not visible. The moulding can be varnished or painted.

Another way to use the moulding is to have it mitred to the size required, then fix it to a base of hardboard with a wood glue. The panel can then be mounted on another piece of hardboard, cut to the size of the inner space, then stuck down firmly in it (b).

Baguette frame: work which has been mounted on thick board, battening or artist's stretchers can have a simple frame made from strips of wood, glued and fixed with panel pins to the sides of the mount. The strips can be mitred or not, as required.

This method would not be suitable for a large panel, as the battening may not be strong enough to take the strain of the stretched fabric.

For large panels, battened hardboard would be stronger, and should not warp. Tack the hardboard to battens, then stretch the fabric and staple, as above.

Mounting on artist's stretchers: wooden stretchers, sold for mounting oil-painting canvas, can be bought in different sizes, and slotted together—they are reasonably priced. Fabric can be stretched and stapled to them, as above.

Mounting in a rigid frame: a carefully chosen outer frame gives emphasis and definition to the work within it. It may be made from wood or metal—there is a very good choice of mouldings available, which can be made to the size required.

Materials needed to mount work in a rigid frame are brads, a small hammer, masking tape, Copydex or UHU, backing card or thin hardboard. Place the mounted panel in the frame. Turn it to the wrong side, and secure it in position with brads, by knocking them at short intervals into the frame, close to the back of the panel. Sometimes the recess is almost taken up, but the brads can usually be inserted (NB: a local picture-framer or DIY shop might do this for you, using a glazier's gun which 'shoots' small triangular pieces of thin metal into the wood.)

Cut a piece of thick card or thin hardboard to fit into the recess, over the brads. Smear glue on to the centre portion of the panel, then press the card backing firmly into place. But if there is no recess left, have the board cut to fit beyond it, resting on the inner edge of the frame. Fix it to the frame with small thin tacks.

'Mock' Frames
There are several ways to simulate a frame, which should be planned to suit the panel.

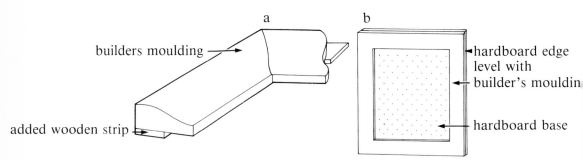

a   b

builders moulding →

added wooden strip →

← hardboard edge level with
← builder's moulding
← hardboard base

Using builder's moulding

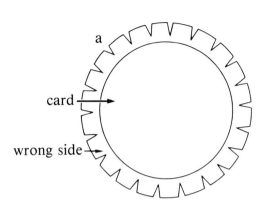

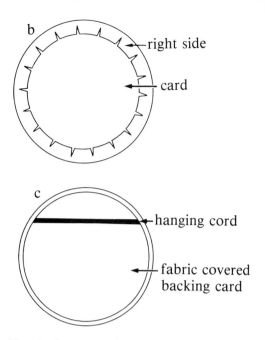

Mounting in a wooden ring

Circular wooden ring: plain wooden rings can be bought from craft shops in a variety of sizes. For this type of framing, choose one with flat, not rounded, edges. Tack the size of the circle on to the background fabric, which should be 5cm larger, and work your embroidery.

Then, using the wooden ring for a pattern, draw round it on to a piece of card. Cut it out, fractionally smaller. Cut another piece of card, fractionally smaller than the first piece, for backing.

Place the larger piece of card on the back of the embroidery, then carefully snip the outer edges of the fabric, near to the card edges (a). Glue the snipped edges of fabric to the card, with UHU or similar glue, and turn the edges to the back of the card, pulling the fabric taut over it (b).

Cover the second piece of card with a matching fabric, for backing. Smear the back of the first circle of card with glue, then press the wrong side of the fabric-covered card to it, matching the edges carefully.

Push the ends of the hanging cord into position, sandwiching them between the two pieces of card approximately 6cm from the top, on opposite sides (c).

Attach the circular frame by smearing glue all round one edge and then pressing it firmly into place over the embroidery, matching the edges.

The backing card can also be stitched to the turned-over edges of the fabric, as well as being glued. For extra neatening, a narrow braid could be glued round the outer edges.

'Half-round' wooden strips: these can be obtained from DIY shops in a variety of widths, and look like split dowel. Have it cut to the size required, and mitred at the corners. Varnish the pieces, then glue them together at the corners. Place into position, then stitch it to the panel, using a strong thread in a matching or contrasting colour, whichever you prefer. Use blanket-stitch, widely spaced, taking it over the dowel, working from the outer edge, so that the connecting bar of the stitch lies on the outer edge. Other stitches can be used, eg herringbone. A small shape of needle-weaving can be worked over each corner, if required.

Split dowel can also be used on the outer edge of a fabric-covered mount (or window mount) or fabric-covered frame, giving an extra dimension and an unusual 'framed' effect.

Split bamboo: suitable for scrims and hessian backgrounds, it varnishes well or can be stained a darker colour. It could be bound at the corners (it need not be mitred), and glued to the panel, or stitched, as described for split dowel.

133

Fabric 'Window' Mounts

These may be varied in shape and size on a basis of hardboard, card or polystyrene, and are a popular method of finishing panels. Basic instructions are given for rectangular and circular 'windows'; the method can be readily adapted for any shape, however irregular. Paper-backed, fabrics can be used.

Polystyrene foam is available in several thicknesses, also as ready-cut tiles. It is easy to cut, but should be handled carefully, as it marks easily, and crumbles. Cut with a sharp blade, held straight, working slowly, to maintain a neat edge. Use a latex adhesive.

First, mount the work on a piece of board, to the size of the required finished panel.

Cut another piece of hardboard, strong card, or polystyrene foam, to the same size, then measure and draw on with a pencil the shape and size of the inner 'window' (a and b).

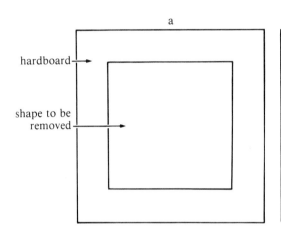
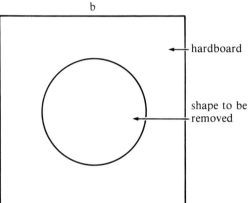

a

hardboard

shape to be removed

b

hardboard

shape to be removed

Making a fabric-covered window mount

'Shady Glade', a small hanging in a mixture of embroidery and weaving techniques, worked on a warp of string. The ground is woven in various green yarns, the lower edge wrapped and whipped. Tree trunks are needlewoven with warp threads cut away to show the backing. The leaves are fabric strips knotted on to the warp. The whole is backed with lightly machine-embroidered dark green fabric. By Moyra McNeill

'High Fliers'. Fabrics and textures are used to depict the mixture of dark and dingy surfaces and splashes of bright colour characteristic of small city gardens. By Sheila Page

Using a sharp craft knife, remove the inner shape, taking care to keep the non-cutting hand away from the path of the blade.

The fabric can be attached to the board, partly or wholly, with adhesive. For a partly glued mount, place the chosen fabric on a clean surface, wrong side uppermost. There should be a good allowance on the outer edge for turning—at least 5cm larger than the board. Place the window mount on the fabric, mark the shape of the inner window to be removed, making it 2cm smaller (use a tailor's pencil). Cut it out, without removing the mount window board (c and d).

Still with the board in position, snip into the corners of the rectangular window mount, stop-

ping short by a fraction. Snip the circle all round, at intervals. Run glue sparingly round the inner edge of the board mount, avoiding the actual edge. Fold the snipped edges over on to the glued edges, pressing firmly and smoothly (e and f).

Turn the mount over on to the right side and place it in position on the panel so that the work shows through. Holding it all firmly in position, turn it over to the wrong side, being careful not to move the mount out of place. The outer edge of the mount can now be finished as in the basic mounting instructions, using either the fabric-backing or the hessian-binding method.

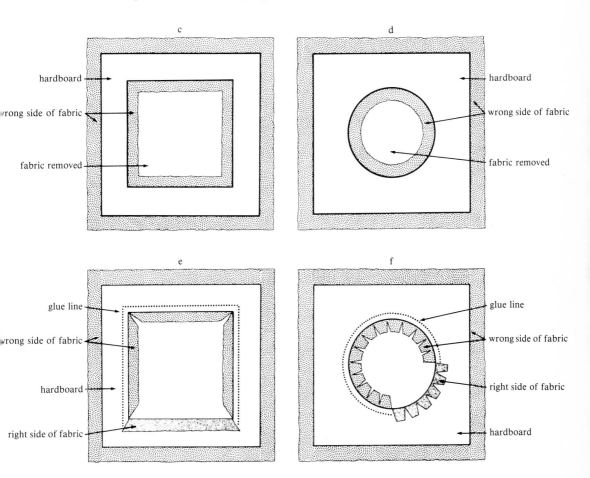

137

For a fully-glued window mount (on hard-board or card, *not* polystyrene), the procedure is slightly different, and some experiment with the chosen fabric should be made on a small piece of scrap board. Using Marvin Medium, stick the trial fabric to the board, and allow to dry. There should be no evidence of the adhesive coming through the fabric—most of them will be success-ful, but it is as well to check first. Paper-backed fabric glues very well and can be stuck with Polycell.

1 Place the fabric (at least 5cm larger than the window mounting board) face-down on a smooth, clean surface.

2 Coat the window mounting board with a thin layer of Marvin Medium, then place it, glue side down, on the fabric, checking it is straight with the fabric grain.

3 Quickly turn the whole of it over, so that the fabric is uppermost. Smooth the fabric carefully over the mount, using a clean soft cloth, making sure there are no wrinkles.

4 Cut away the centre portion of fabric, leaving a 2cm margin to turn over on to the board.

5 Turn the mount over again, so that the board is uppermost. Spread a thin line of glue on the inner edge of the mount, and press the inner margin of fabric over on to it.

6 Trim away surplus fabric at the outer edge.

7 Proceed with finishing, as in basic mount-ing, using either fabric backing or hessian-binding finish (page 128).

Other Window Mounts

Wood veneer: this is suitable only for an un-glazed panel. The wood veneer is mounted to fit exactly on a hardboard window mount—the outer edge should be the same size as the rigid outer frame. Give it a coat of clear varnish. By matching the outer frame, veneered mount and worked panel, a satisfying unity can be achieved (see 'Young Rhino', Project 13, page 166).

Plywood: thinner plywood can be cut with a sharp knife, treating edges carefully as they can easily be damaged. Thicker plywood can be cut at a do-it-yourself shop. It varnishes easily, giving an effective finish.

Cork: tiles and table mats can be cut easily. They look better with several coats of varnish (see 'Brown Owl', Project 8, page 156).

Mounting card: this is used extensively for

Several window mounts

pictures, and is available in a good range of colours. It is improved by a bevelled cut edge, which can be done by a local picture-framer. Card can also be painted.

'Gourd' Project

A project much enhanced by unusual mounting is described here in detail as it may give further ideas for mounting other designs. Pulled work is combined with quilting to form the gourd design.

1 Coarse scrim is pulled into a series of holes of different sizes, not working to any definite de-sign.

2 A contrasting bright, shiny orange fabric is placed underneath, and the pulled spaces mar-ked on the fabric with a tailor's pencil.

3 The orange fabric is tacked to a thin cotton sheeting, and the spaces quilted with backstitch, by hand, using a dark orange thread.

4 Padding is added to the spaces by slitting the cotton backing, stuffing with kapok, then stitching up the slit with a few overcasting stitches.

5 Beads are stitched round some of the spaces.

6 For mounting, a paper pattern of a gourd is cut out, large enough to take in all the em-broidery.

7 The gourd shape is cut out from a piece of thin hardboard (original 50cm square), making a window mount.

8 The scrim is then glued to the *outside* of the hardboard, being stretched over the cut-out shape, with all the worked area showing through the space.

'Field and Flowers'. Machine and hand embroidery on a sprayed background, with painted card surround. The mounts and frame are an integral part of the design and were carefully thought out beforehand. Thin sections of card are closely wrapped with silk threads harmonising with the colours used in the design. By *Verina Warren* (Embroiderers' Guild)

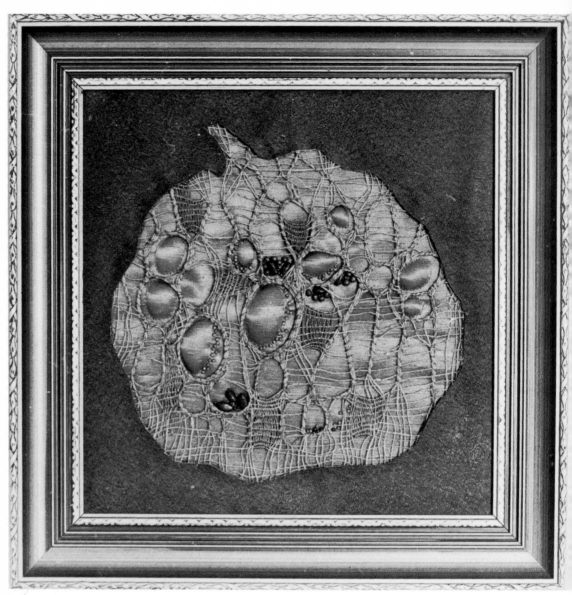

9 Using a piece of brown leatherette (to fit the hardboard, ie 50cm) the gourd shape is cut out, as in the hardboard, then glued to it, with the scrim sandwiched between and showing through the leatherette cut-out shape.

10 The orange quilted fabric is then glued to the *back* of the hardboard, with the quilting positioned to show through the scrim and the leatherette.

11 The panel is then completed with a carefully chosen dull gold frame, as described in the section on framed panels.

'Gourd'. Coarse scrim, worked separately with overcasting and needleweaving, is on a hand-quilted shiny orange background fabric. Behind the largest holes in the scrim the background is stuffed, with small beads added and some larger, hand-made clay beads. A window mount was cut from thin hardboard, then covered with brown leatherette, and completed with a gold frame (see text)

140

Wooden Oval Mounts

An attractive oval shape can be cut from a thick piece of wood, eg blockboard (nearly 2cm thick) which is often available as an offcut. If you provide a pattern of the shape, a DIY shop will cut it for you.

The mounting can be done in two slightly different ways: by glueing the fabric to the back of the wood, then neatening with a backing fabric, or by fixing the fabric to the sides of the wood with glue and small tacks, then glueing a matching braid over them. The back of the wood could be varnished, or left plain.

Irregular-shaped Panels (see 'Beachcomb', page 105).

Panels can be mounted on board or card cut to any irregular shape. Make a paper pattern (use newspaper) then draw round it on the selected board, and cut it out, using a sharp craft knife or small fretsaw.

When mounting on irregular shapes, remember to snip any curves to avoid wrinkles. Should these occur and look unsightly, cover them with a matching braid or binding. This is better stitched to the edge nearest the top of the panel, and glued on the lower edge.

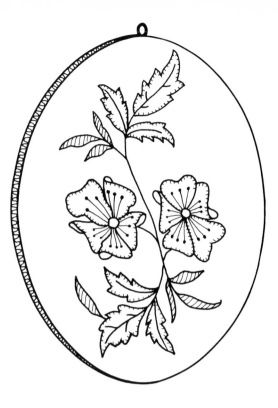

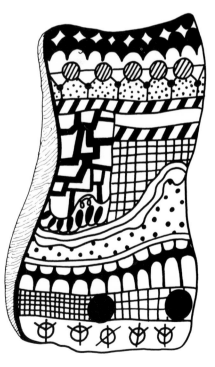

141

'Sheep' by Karyn Prowen. Embroidery and appliqué on canvas, using knitting and weaving wools, sheepskin and woollen material, make up this very strokable hanging. The horns are stuffed leather and suede. (Embroiderers' Guild)

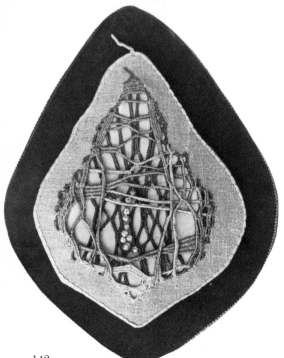

Two shaped mounts emphasise the shape of 'Pear', worked in needleweaving and whipped threads on a delicate sage-green hessian bordered with a thick couched thread. The outer mount is of dark green furnishing velvet, edged with green braid and lined with matching green satin for a backing. A curtain-ring is stitched to it for hanging

142

GLAZED PANELS

Panels placed under glass are protected from general wear and tear, but a certain amount of texture is lost, which must be taken into consideration. For delicate work, and free fabric collage where the edges of the fabric are untreated, glazing is often the best treatment. Many other types of work can be glazed, but if there is a raised surface the frame must be deeper to accommodate it behind the glass.

Glass is obtainable in several different grades. Picture glass is thin and lightweight; window glass could be used, but is heavier and thicker. Non-reflective glass has a slightly grainy appearance, which looks attractive on some work, not on other kinds. Perspex can be used as an alternative to glass, if it suits the work. There are several different ways of glazing panels.

Rigid Frame

This is the familiar 'picture' type presentation, which can be made up with or without an inner window mount. As a window mount usually improves the presentation, it is a good idea to include one, if it suits the work. It can be picture-mounting card, or fabric-covered card. (Ready-cut mounts can be bought, with a square, round or oval window.)

1 Decide on the size of the finished panel. Then choose the frame, and have the hardboard mounting board (thin), the inner window mount and the glass all cut to fit at the same time. It is not advisable to mount the panel and then later order the frame; it might not fit correctly, which would be time-consuming and expensive to rectify. The mounting board should only fit loosely in the frame at this stage, before the fabric is mounted on it.

2 Work on a clean surface, with enough room to accommodate everything. Clean and wipe the glass carefully, checking that it is free from smears. Place the frame face down, put the glass into it, then add the window mount, if used, then the panel face down. Then, holding the frame and panel firmly together, turn it over, and inspect it for specks of dust.

3 Turn it over again, and fix the panel firmly in place by knocking brads into the recess of the frame or having diamond points fitted with a glazier's gun.

4 Finish the back by fitting a piece of card or thin hardboard into the recess. Then cover the

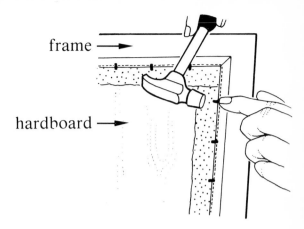

frame ➝

hardboard ➝

Mounting in a rigid frame

edges with masking tape, or brown gummed paper. If there is no room to fit card into the recess, have the board cut to fit beyond it, nearly to the edge of the frame itself, then fix it to the frame with a few small screws. Tacks can be used, if the glass is protected on a pad of thick blanket, but there is always a risk that the glass will crack.

5 To hang the panel, insert screw-eyes approximately a third of the way down from the top of the frame. They should be chosen the correct size for the frame—small ones for light narrow frames, thicker ones for large heavy panels.

6 Attach nylon hanging cord, used double for heavy panels.

Conservation Glazing

More care is taken with this method that the textile does not touch the glass and dust is excluded. It should be considered for work which may become a family heirloom. Conservation board could be used for delicate fabrics. It is acid-free, and available from some art shops.

1 Obtain frame, glass, hardboard, and a narrow fillet of wood (mitred) to fit between the glass and the textile. (Alternatively, a window mount can be cut from balsa wood, covered with fabric, and used instead of a fillet.) Check that they will all fit into the frame, as some frames do not have a very wide recess.

2 Mount the work on to hardboard (ordinary card is not recommended, as it may contain acid which could harm the fabric).

3 Clean the glass carefully. It can be rubbed with anti-static polish (Perspex polish no 3). Insert it into the frame, then seal it into place

with Tuftape, using a narrow margin on the glass so that it does not show through the frame moulding.

4 Fit the fillet into place, or place the window mount in position.

5 Insert the mounted work. Turn right side up, and check that there are no specks on the glass.

6 Fix into place with brads. Glue brown paper over the back of hardboard and brads. Seal edges with Tuftape.

7 Fix screw-eyes and hanging cord.

Fabric-mounted Glass

This is a new method: the glass is held firmly in place by the fabric window mount. It works well on small panels, particularly with a circular 'window'. It is important to ensure that the fixed hanging rings do not show through the work on the right side when the window mount is in position.

1 Decide on outer measurements, eg 20cm × 20cm. Then cut the glass, or have it cut, and a strong backing card, exactly to the size.

2 Deal with the card backing first. Fix two small hanging rings fairly near the top and the outer edges.

3 Mount your work on the card (with rings on the outer side), glueing on the edges of the card. Do not take the fabric over the edges of the card. Pull taut, removing all wrinkles. Trim the edges of the fabric level with the card.

4 Clean the glass, place it over the mounted work, and using a thin, self-adhesive parcel tape, bind the edges of the glass to the card.

5 Prepare another piece of card for the window mount. Cut the outer edges exactly the same size as the glass. Remove a 'window' shape from it—circular, oval, irregular. Cover it with fabric as explained in the section on panels and window mounts. Deal with the cut-out window shape only, allowing approximately 5cm extra fabric for turning on the outer edges.

6 Place fabric-mounted card on top of the glass, matching the edges of the glass exactly. Holding it all together, turn it over and lay it face-down on a clean surface.

7 Glue the fabric to the back of the card, pulling it taut, and checking on the right side that all wrinkles are out. The corners can be mitred, but do not trim away too much at the corners in case the tension pulls it out of position.

8 Trim away excess fabric, leaving a glued margin of approximately 3cm.

9 Cover all the raw edges of the fabric with self-adhesive tape, or a wide brown-paper strip (see 'Baby Owl', page 158).

Clipped Glass

No rigid outer frame is used with this type of presentation—the glass and boards are held together with clips. It is ideal for flat, delicate work, or for work which does not require mounting on a board first to stretch it.

1 Mount the work on strong card, taking the fabric to the back of the card, and glueing the edges down neatly. If the work does not require stretching, prepare a background for it—either a coloured card, etc, or a fabric-covered card. A window mount could also be incorporated.

2 Cut glass and backing board to the required size—a thick backing board should be used, eg chipboard, to take screws in the sides or at the back. Clean the glass carefully and place the work in position. Secure it if necessary with a few stitches, or a small amount of adhesive. Place glass, and mount if used, in position—check for specks of dust, etc.

3 Using special clips and screws, secure the glass to the board, placing two on each side, and top and bottom.

4 Fix screw-eyes to the back of the board, and hang with nylon hanging cord.

An alternative method is to use a thinner backing board, and screwless clips (Emo). If using this method, be sure to fix the hanging rings to the backing board *before* clipping to the glass.

Perspex

Perspex has some interesting possibilities, particularly as it can be cut into shapes, and holes drilled in it, with care (place a piece of Sellotape over the position of the hole). Some work is enhanced with light shining through it, and two layers of perspex would be one way of mounting to achieve this effect. They could be fixed with clips, with a rigid frame, or laced together through holes drilled at intervals.

Perspex is available in several different thicknesses.

Passepartout edging

This is a quick and inexpensive method of glazing a panel. It is not generally used for work which has taken a long time to do, but it is useful for items which have been executed quickly, for a small gift, etc—the method seems most suitable for small-sized work. A window mount can be used.

1 Have glass, mounting card and backing board (thick card) cut to required size.

2 Obtain two passepartout rings, which have a small staple to fix into the backing board. It is important that these rings are put into position before the rest of the mounting is done. Fix them into the card a third of the way down from the top and 3–5cm in from each side, depending on the size of the panel. Stick a small piece of masking tape over them.

3 If the fabric is thin, it can be neatly glued to the back of the mounting board. If the fabric is thick, glue to the extreme edges of the card, on the right side, and stick the work down, pulling the fabric taut. Trim off the surplus fabric, close to the edge of the card.

4 Clean the glass and place it over the work. It should be exactly aligned with the backing card underneath, with the window mount in position if used.

5 Using passepartout in the colour required, cut four strips for the sides, and place them in position on the glass (dealing with two opposite sides first). The passepartout should be fixed half on the upper side (the glass) and half on the lower side (the backing board). Take it to the top and bottom of each side, then trim off, close to the edge.

Shadow-box

Work requiring greater depth between the glass and the backing can be mounted in a shadow-box. This is constructed with fillets of wood cut to the depth required, then fixed up against the frame, with the glass above and the backing board underneath. A picture framer or handyman should be able to construct it (see photo).

Experiments can be made with different types of boxes and wooden drawers, etc. Perspex could be fitted instead of glass.

Hockey-stick frame

This is another type of frame used when depth is required. It derives its name from the fact that the wooden frame, in section, resembles a hockey stick. Fillets of wood, or another narrow frame, are used to keep the glass in place and secure the panel. The mouldings available are limited, both in materials and design, which could be a drawback.

10 Hangings to Make

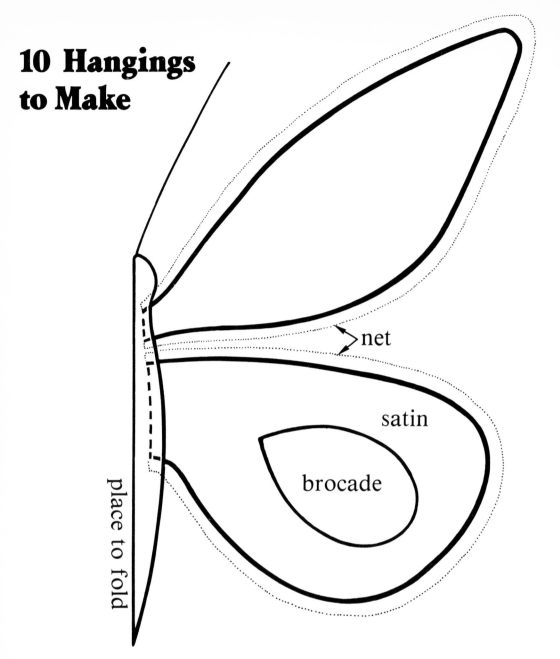

place to fold

net

satin

brocade

PROJECT 1 BUTTERFLY

Fabric collage, made up as a glazed panel. Original 31 × 38cm.

A fabric collage placed under glass is quick to make, as the raw edges do not have to be neatened. Ideal for beginners.

Requirements

White background fabric, 26 × 35cm

Blue mounting fabric 34 × 41cm

Thin strong card for mounting white fabric, 23 × 32cm .

Thin hardboard for mounting blue fabrics, 30 × 37cm

Narrow white frame, with glass, 31 × 38cm

1½ metres narrow white lace

Small pieces of satin, organza and net, in blues

Small print fabric for body

Blue threads. Black Lurex for antennae

UHU glue; (PVA if possible for lace)

Method

1 Take two tracings of the butterfly pattern.
2 Using one of the tracings, cut into sections, as indicated, and use them for patterns, cutting out wings—top in organza, lower in satin. Also four in net (allow a small overlap, to fit under body).
3 Cut body in patterned fabric.
4 Tack a centre line on the white fabric.
5 Tack the fabric wings into position. The base of the top wings should be halfway down the centre line. Use the tracing to check position.
6 Couch a thread on the wings, as shown in the photograph. The lower wings have a large spot added, with a small shape of extra net.
7 Place the net over the wings, overlapping the fabrics. Catch-stitch, centrally, on the body area.
8 Tack body over base of wings, neatening edges with a couched thread.

'Butterfly': couched knobbly wool adds definition to the wings and the body is made of printed corduroy, the wings of voile and nets, all in shades of blue. White lace stitched to the inner mount adds delicacy and breaks the line of the white background and the darker blue outer mount. Put under glass, the fabrics are flattened, giving the butterfly a pressed look

9 Couch a black Lurex thread for antennae.
10 Mount the collage over card, glueing edges to the back and pulling fabric taut.
11 Mount the blue fabric on the hardboard, glueing the edges to the back and pulling fabric taut.
12 Glue the white fabric collage, centrally, on the blue mounted fabric.
13 Attach the white lace to the white mounted collage, using a very light smear of PVA (which should dry colourless—make a small test to check). If no PVA is available, slip-stitch it invisibly into place.
14 Finish framing, as in glazed panel section.

147

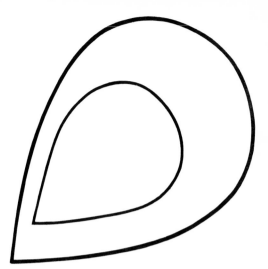

PROJECT 2 PEONY

Fabric collage. Original 32 × 39cm. A simple flower head gives scope for using a variety of fabrics, threads and beads. It is quickly worked, and can be mounted simply or framed in a number of the ways given in this book. Ideal for beginners.

Requirements

Small pieces of fabrics in shades of one colour, eg pink
Dark background fabric (eg dark green), 5cm larger than the hardboard (below)
Green fabric for leaves
Threads, braids, beads, to match colour of petals
Hardboard, 32 × 39cm

Method

1 Cut five large petal shapes and arrange them on the top half of the fabric. Cut three in tulle, and place over three petals. Pin down, overlapping some, the points meeting at the centre.
2 Cut five inner petals from different fabrics, adding velvet, satin, etc. Tack into position over the other petals.
3 Cut a stem from cord or wool, and stitch it down, curving it.
4 Cut a small circle of lace (white in the original) and tack it over the centre, where the petals and stem meet.
5 Now embellish the petal edges with couched thread, braids, etc, or stitchery, eg herringbone, cretan. A machine stitch can also be used.
6 Cut a small centre from velvet, brocade, etc, allowing a small turning. Tuck the turnings in, and catch-stitch the centre piece over the lace.
7 Add a few beads and sequins.
8 Cut two leaf shapes, pin and tack them into position. Sew them down with stitchery or machine zig-zag.
9 Glue the finished work to the back of the hardboard, as in basic mounting. Other mounting methods can be used if preferred.

Peony collage, a first effort, quickly made with hand and machine stitching. Fabrics in shades of pink, from pale nets to dark velvets, on dark green background

PROJECT 3 SEA SHELLS

A collection of small items can be displayed on a panel, and instead of shells you could use feathers, fossils, beads, keys or buttons. Only basic stitches are used—children would find this an interesting holiday project.

Requirements

Length of petersham ribbon or similar. Original 36cm × 6cm
1 metre braid
Hardboard, 9cm × 41cm
Fabric to cover hardboard front and back—hessian, etc 30cm × 50cm
Curtain ring
Collection of items
Threads

Method

1 Arrange items on petersham ribbon, leaving a space at top and bottom. Tack into place.
2 Embroider around them, taking threads over them to hold in place, if necessary. Several rows of blanket stitch, pulled together, will hold shells in place if they do not have a hole. Stitches used on the original are fly, cretan, blanket, chain and French knots.
3 Cut a piece from the fabric, 13cm × 46cm, then tack the shape of the hardboard, centrally, on it.
4 Tack the ribbon exactly in the centre of it, then stitch it down by hand or machine.
5 Tack the braid in place over the edges of the embroidered ribbon, then stitch down by hand or machine.
6 Place hardboard into position on the back of the work, and glue fabric edges over it, pulling the fabric taut.
7 Cut another piece of fabric to neaten the back, 12cm × 45cm. Tack turnings (2cm) and slip-stitch into place on back of work, adjusting turning if necessary.
8 Stitch a curtain ring to the centre back edge of the work, 4 cm from the top, for hanging.

'Sea Shells'

150

PROJECT 4 FEATHER

Surface stitchery panel (basic mounting). Original 22 × 58cm. The short lines of the feather are ideal for working a wide variety of stitches quickly.

Requirements

Background fabric—velvet, wool, etc
Variety of wools, threads and cottons
Piece of thick mounting board (any type) in size required
Backing fabric or hessian binding (for neatening back)

Method

1 Cut a paper shape to the size required, ensuring that a space is left at top, bottom and sides when placed on background fabric. Draw in the vein line.
2 Pin on to the background fabric; tack round the shape, then on the vein line, through the paper. Pull away the paper carefully.
3 Stitch the vein line, first, with chain stitch; work one single line, then another close to it, tapering it at the top, leaving a single line. Work this stitch loosely so that the fabric is not pulled. (There is no need for a frame.)
4 Work a variety of stitches on the left side, which is the widest. Make sure they curve upwards slightly, not going out at right angles in a straight line. Take the stitches as far as the tacking lines, but otherwise the actual outline is not clearly defined. This gives a more natural look.
5 A few spaces are filled in with small glass beads and bugle beads for added interest.
6 The narrow side of the feather is filled in with long straight stitches, in a thin thread or wool, and a line of crested chain stitch.

Basic mounting

7 Cover one side of the mounting board with a piece of old blanket or other spare fabric. Place the work on top, positioning the board correctly, then turn it over on to a clean surface. Continue mounting as in basic mounting procedure (page 128), neatening the back with a matching fabric or using the hessian binding method. (Narrow panels are sometimes easier to finish with the fabric method.)
8 Fix a small curtain ring to the centre top edge of the back of the panel.

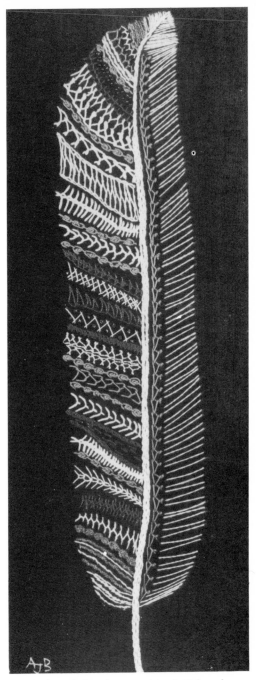

'Feather', worked to show a variety of stitches—here including cretan, herringbone, knotted cable chain, vandyke, fly and crested chain, in different threads. The simple straight stitches on the right add emphasis to the stitches opposite. Worked on brown velvet and mounted on lightweight insulation board. By Audrey Babington (Ian Robson)

151

'Silver Stars'

PROJECT 5 SILVER STARS

The embroidered inner section is attached to a lampshade ring, covered with blue net, giving the illusion of hanging in space. Quickly worked, and a suitable project for children, though help may be needed to attach the net to the wire frame.

Requirements

Wire lampshade ring 30cm diameter
Circle of blue net, 34cm diameter
Thick card, 20cm diameter
Dark blue fabric, 24cm diameter (rayon lining material or similar)
Wadding (or old blanket)
Thin card, 19cm diameter (blue if possible)
Sequins, beads, etc
Curtain rings
Silver and pale blue threads, plus dark blue for outer stitching
Blue raffine or thread
Ring frame

Method

1 Tack round the thick card circle on to the dark blue fabric. Fix it into the ring frame.
2 Work a design of star shapes—some with thread-covered curtain rings, filled with sequins, beads, etc, with radiating stitches. Single sequins are scattered at random, with three or four straight stitches in a thin thread.

3 Cover card with a thin layer of interlining—wadding or old blanket. Glue lightly, cutting off the surplus level with the edges of the card circle.
4 Take the embroidered fabric out of the ring frame. Place the wadding side of the card on the back of the embroidery, then glue the edges of the fabric to it, snipping at intervals, and pull it taut (a).
5 Glue the thin card circle to the back of the mounted embroidery, to neaten.
6 Prepare the outer ring: wind the blue raffine or thread, tightly round, completely to cover the wire. Secure the end with a dab of glue.
7 Tack the blue net to the ring, turning over the edges, then machine-stitch it close to the edge, using a zip foot attachment and matching cotton (b).
8 Place the embroidered inner circle in position on the net circle, then catch-stitch it into place with small neat stitches and matching cotton.
9 Work a bold connecting thread, zig-zag fashion, stitching through the inner circle, and taking it over the wire and through the back so that all the stitching is on the front of the net.

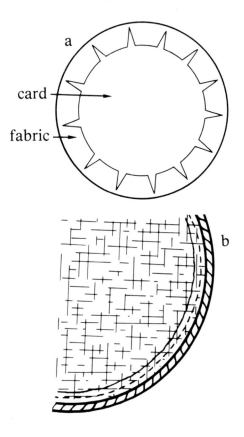

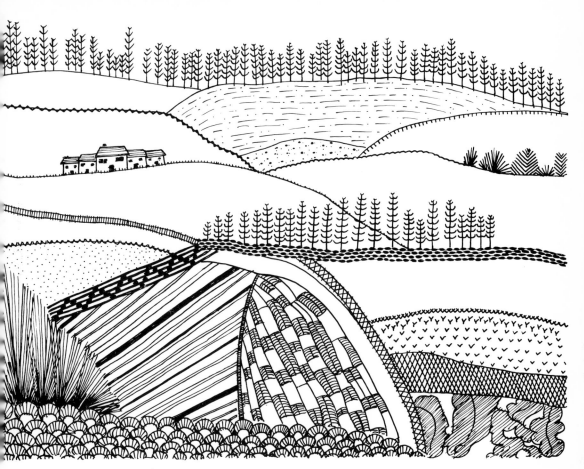

PROJECT 6 APPLIQUÉ LANDSCAPE

Appliqué and stitchery panel. Fields of simple shapes are made from a variety of fabrics—wool, velvet, corduroy, etc. This appliqué method can be used for any landscape. Make sure there is some feature of interest, such as a building or a group of trees. The panel has a double fabric mount.

Requirements

Selection of small pieces of fabric
Pale blue fabric for background, 50 × 60cm
Dark blue fabric for outer mount, 56 × 66cm
Selection of threads, including textured wools
Hardboard (thin) for appliqué, 40 × 50cm
Hardboard (medium) for outer mount, 46 × 56cm
Iron-on Vilene

Method

1 Using a sheet of drawing-paper 6cm larger than the finished appliqué (46 × 56cm), draw the fields, buildings, trees, etc.
2 Take *two* tracings of the drawing—one to be cut into pattern pieces for the appliqué fabrics, the other to be used as a check for the design: place it over the work as the fabrics are put into place.
3 Give all the field shapes a letter or number.
4 Cut out the field shapes from one sheet, and use these shapes as templates for the fabrics, allowing a small overlap on the lower edges and at the sides of the landscape (see drawing). If any of the fabrics tend to fray, iron them on to the Vilene.
5 Lay the blue background fabric flat on a clean surface. Pin all the field shapes into position, starting at the top and overlapping them. Use the other tracing to check positions, placing it over the top of the work as it

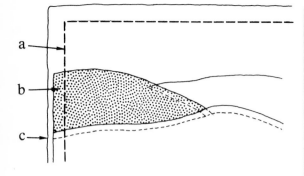

progresses. Tack the fields into place, keeping all the fabrics flat.

7 Secure them to the background using a mixture of stitchery, eg fly stitch, herringbone, couching, with braids and textured wools. One field in the foreground could have some needle-weaving worked over the fabric to give added texture, and some coarse dark lace for hedges.

9 Add the other details, eg houses, bushes, in simple straight stitches. Trees are fly stitches in a variety of thin threads on the skyline—dark blue, purple, black and grey.

To mount

10 Place the appliqué face-down on a clean surface, then put the smaller piece of hardboard (40 × 50cm) in position on the wrong side of the work. Turn it all over to check position: there should be approximately 3cm of appliqué, plus a little more of background fabric, to overlap the board.

11 Glue the edges of the work to the back of the hardboard, pulling it taut. Continue as for double mounting, neatening with fabric or the hessian binding method. Use the large piece of hardboard and dark blue fabric for the outer mount.

'Lighthouse', a large panel in fabric collage, with simple stitchery, based on an advertising illustration. The lighthouse, on grey blanket over card, was worked separately, then applied to the background over a light-halo of nets. Sequin waste and silver lamé catch the light effectively in the tower. Mounted on Plaschem, a very lightweight board. A design suitable for a boy's room, a school hall, etc

154

PROJECT 7 LIGHTHOUSE

Collage panel (basic mounting). Original 122 × 60cm. A large panel mounted on light-weight board. The simple shapes are easy to assemble.

Requirements

Dark blue or black background fabric, with a slight sheen, cut 10cm larger than original, or to size required.
Grey blanket, or other fabric, for lighthouse and rocks
Brown sequin mesh, or similar, for light cage, plus yellow fabric
Dark brown leather or felt for triangular top
Light chiffon, or similar, for waves
White tulle for light halo
A few white beads for spray
A piece of insulation board (lightweight), 122 × 60cm, or chosen size
Hessian binding for neatening back
UHU glue

Method

1. Cut a paper pattern to sizes given, or to fit chosen measurements. Cut the lighthouse shape from thick card.
2. Cover the main shape with the grey fabric by glueing the edges to the back of the shape (cardboard).
3. Work blanket stitch over the shape, using dark grey wool or other thread, and graduating the stitches—small at the top, larger at the base. Take the stitches to the sides, concealing any ends at the back of the shape.
4. Cover the light cage with two fabrics—first a yellow one, with a sheen if possible, then brown sequin mesh. Glue the edges of the pieces to the back of the card shapes.
5. Cover the triangular top with brown leather or felt. (The original had anodised leather cut from an old fashion boot.)
6. Slip-stitch the sections together, then stitch a narrow braid over the joins.
7. Cover the base mounting board with the dark blue fabric, taking the edges to the back and glueing them down. Pull the fabric taut over the board.
8. Cut two tulle circles, 34 and 24cm diameter, and tack them into position (see photograph). Radiate long straight stitches, using a thin silk or cotton thread.

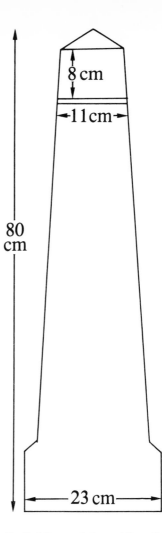

9. Glue the lighthouse into position, then stitch edges to the background to hold secure.
10. Cut some rock shapes in card, then cover with the grey fabric, padding them slightly.
11. Fix the rocks to the background, then stitch the chiffon between them, for waves. Add a few beads for spray.
12. Neaten the back with the hessian binding method.

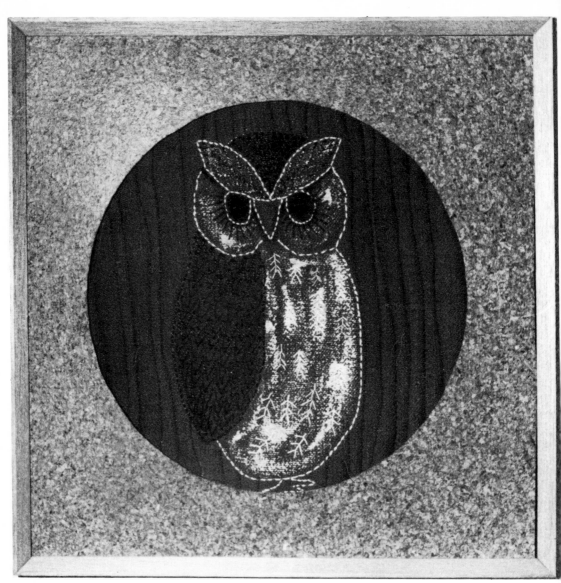

PROJECT 8 BROWN OWL

Hand-quilted owl on machine-quilted ground, with fabric painting. Original 29cm square. A cork tile (varnished) is used for a window mount.

Requirements

Fabric 35cm square, or adapt measurements to your requirements (medium-brown jersey-wool fabric was used for the original, but any closely woven fabric, including velvet, will do, or something with a sheen on it)

White fabric paint for the body (not essential)

Threads—coton-à-broder or stranded cottons

'Brown Owl'. Hand and machine quilting, combined with white fabric paint and simple stitchery on light brown jersey wool

(chestnut-brown and dark brown, white for body outline). Bronze Lurex thread (Twilley's) for ears

Black felt for eyes

Wadding and thin cotton backing, 29cm square

Cork tile, 29cm diameter

Simple wooden frame, 29cm square

Hardboard (thin) to fit in frame

Frame for working

156

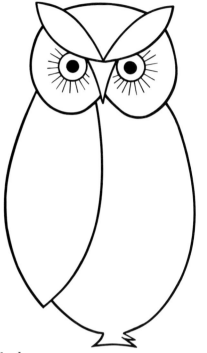

Method

1 Draw the owl, 18cm from top of head to bottom of feet, 10·5cm across at widest point, or draw it to your chosen measurements. In this drawing it is shown half-size. Then transfer it to the fabric, using a prick-and-pounce method, or else by tacking lines through the tracing paper.

2 Using white fabric paint, paint the body and round the face (not the eyes). Leave some of the background fabric showing through. Iron on the back to fix the colour.

3 Tack a circle 21cm diameter (if using measurements of the original) round the owl—the size of the cork window mount you intend to use.

4 Tack the top fabric to the thin cotton backing, sandwiching the wadding between them. Fix them in a frame, a ring or an old picture frame.

5 Using the white thread, backstitch the body, nose, eyes, face and ears, pulling the thread slightly.

6 Using dark brown thread, backstitch the wing and top of head.

7 Stitch black felt circles for eyes. Add a radiating half-circle of blanket stitch round the white stitching of the eyes.

8 Using chestnut thread, add V-shaped lines of chain stitch, filling in the top of the head.

9 Using the two shades of brown, work alternate rows of fly stitches on the wing.

10 Using white thread, work blocks of fly stitch (working with the body upside-down). Vary the number in the blocks.

11 Using copper Lurex thread, work feather stitch on the ears.

12 Stitch the background, using a dark brown Sylko cotton. Machine uneven rows, making lines representing the bark of a tree. Start working from the owl, outwards to the edges of the tacked circle and just beyond.

13 Pull all the loose ends of thread to the back of the work and knot them together.

To mount

14 Varnish the cork tile with a coat of polyurethane matt or semi-gloss varnish, and leave it to dry.

15 Mark a circle of 21cm diameter in pencil on the back of the tile (use a plate, if no compasses are available).

16 Using a sharp craft knife, carefully cut away the marked circle.

17 Remove the tacking threads from the machine-quilted fabric, then cut away the excess wadding which extends from the machining to the edge of the fabrics. This will allow the cork window-mount to lie flat.

18 Glue the work to the hardboard edges, *not* turning the fabric over to the back of it. Trim away overlapping fabric, cutting it close to the edges of the hardboard.

19 Place the cork window-mount in position over the quilting, with the owl showing through.

20 Put them in the frame, and secure with brads; then neaten with masking tape or sticky brown-paper strip.

21 Fix screw eyes and hanging cord.

'Baby Owl', traced from wrapping-paper, and hand stitched on a pale fawn cotton background, with an orange cotton fabric mount.

PROJECT 9 BABY OWL

Appliqué. Fabric-mounted glazed panel. Original 18 × 18cm. The appliqué is very easy and quickly worked, but the mounting needs care with the measurements.

Requirements

Small pieces of white, brown and black felt
Short length of brown wool; brown and black stranded cottons
Pale fawn background fabric, 23 × 23cm
Dull orange or brown fabric, 23 × 23cm
Glass, 18 × 18cm
Strong card, 18 × 18cm
Hanging cord
UHU glue

Method

1 Draw owl pattern pieces—in these drawings they are shown full-size—and cut main body in white felt, head, wing, eyes and tail in brown felt, nose in black felt.
2 Tack into position, centrally, on fawn fabric, placing white body first, overlaying the others.
3 Embroider fly stitches in thin brown cotton thread on body. With double thread, work a line of chain stitch from A to B.

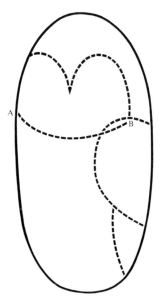

4 Embroider detached chain stitches on wing, and stem stitches on tail, with double brown thread.
5 Work two rows of chain stitch, with double brown thread, round body edges.
6 Stitch eyes into place, and add a dark sequin in centre with black cotton (single thread).

7 Couch the brown wool at the base of the owl, to make a branch.
8 Make up as for fabric-mounted glass—see page 144.

PROJECT 10 **PATCHWORK HANGING**

Designed by Alice Timmins. The different blocks are made up separately, lined, then seamed together. See colour photograph on page 67.

Requirements

A variety of cotton fabrics, some plain
Heavyweight Vilene
Thin cotton fabric for lining (toning colour)
Patchwork templates
Card for mounting
Graph paper, if available
Sewing cottons
Metal ring

Method

1 Cut the Vilene shapes overleaf (which are left in the patchwork):
Top block—6 triangles (a)
Second block—25 squares (b)
Third block—5 diamonds (c)
Fourth block—9 oblongs (d)
Fifth block—3 'coffins' (e) and 4 triangles (f)
Sixth block—5 oblongs (g)
Seventh block—3 long triangles (h)
Eighth block—20 hexagons (i) and 18 small diamonds (j)
Ninth block—12 small diamonds (j)

2 Pin Vilene shapes on fabrics (with grain straight) and cut them out, with turnings.
3 Tack fabrics over Vilene, folding corners neatly.
4 Seam patchwork blocks together, following the sequence in the illustration.
5 Mount each block on firm card to give a good shape: using the relevant template (eg for the top block a triangle (a)) and graph paper, if available, draw round it, forming the shape of the block. Cut the shape in card.
6 Use the card shape to cut the lining material, adding turnings. Tack the material to the card, turning the fabric edges over the card.
7 Pin this card lining to the block, wrong sides together. Oversew the edges together, using matching cotton.
8 Seam the various blocks together, to give the shape on the illustration. Remove all tackings.
9 Cover the metal ring with a bias strip of fabric, and stitch to the top block.

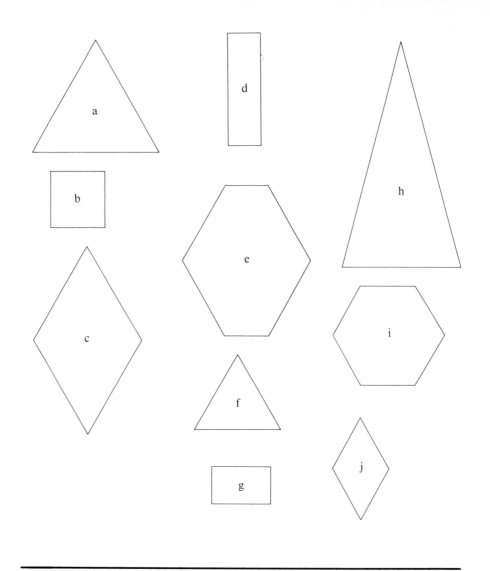

PROJECT 11 THE FAMILY

Designed by Herta Puls. Original 36 × 60cm. A soft hanging worked in five layers of cotton fabric, using the Kuna Indian mola appliqué technique. It can be worked to any size, and the family number varied.

Requirements

Five pieces of thin cotton fabric, in different colours (original is in red, violet, orange, black and brown)
Exactly matching sewing cottons

(right) 'The Family'. Thin fabrics in clear, bright colours, usually contrasted with a dark colour, give best results with this technique

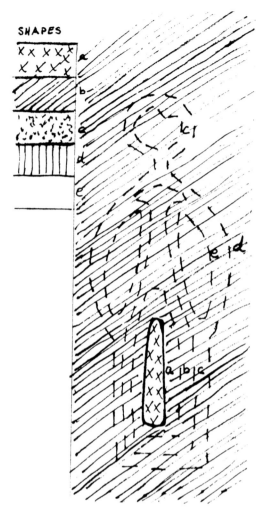

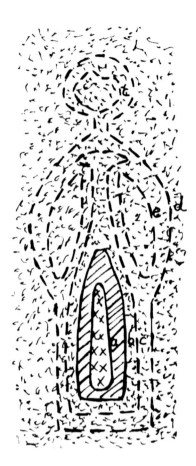

Method

1 Take base layer (red) and cover it with second layer (violet), with the grain running in the same direction. Pin together.

2 Trace the figures given in the sketches, marking in all the lines, or adapt the sizes to suit. The different forms of shading given in the key indicate the different colours of fabric. Make your own choice, but in these instructions it is assumed that you are following the original scheme.

3 Using fine pins, pin the tracing in position, then tack through all the lines, using a *contrasting* cotton. Remove tracing carefully—this can be done most easily by slitting the paper under each stitch *only*, with a sharp pin. The paper will then lift off.

4 Cut the top layer inside shape with a seam allowance, snip through the tacking threads of line a, and lift the fabric carefully, leaving tufts in place.

5 Turn under seam allowance to tacking tufts, and sew with invisible hemstitches in cotton thread, matching second layer on line a through both layers (drawing 1). (Snip any curved edges so they lie flat, throughout the work.)

6 Cover work with a third layer (orange). On the *back* of the work the stitches should be exactly on the tacking tufts. (The remaining tacking lines show the other areas to be worked.) Repeat the tacking lines b–e from the back.

7 Cut the third layer (orange) *inside* shape b

162

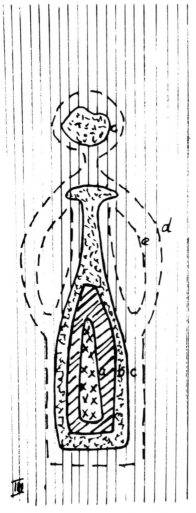

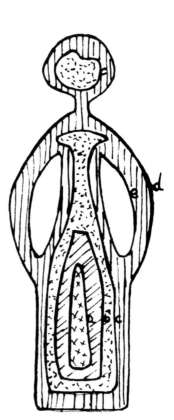

with a seam allowance, and work on line b.

8 Cover the work with the fourth layer (black). From the back of the work, re-tack lines c, d and e. Cut the black layer *inside* shape c for the face. Work as above, always matching the cotton to the top layer, and keeping the grain of the fabrics running in the same direction.

9 Remove inner surplus fabric. Add the top layer (brown). Tack from the back lines d and e, and around shapes d and e.

10 Cut the brown layer with seam allowance inside d and stitch neatly.

11 Cut the brown layer *outside* shape e, turn under the edges, and stitch on line e around shape e.

12 Remove all tacking threads.

Sketches by Herta Puls for her hanging showing 'The Family'

When working, the detailed instructions have to be followed on each layer of fabric for each figure. The bands of colour should be narrow—large, wide bands tend to pucker.

13 Finish the work by turning the sides over and catch-stitching to the back. The top and bottom edges are frayed to show all the layers of colour. The original is mounted on a piece of clear Perspex, 5cm larger than the hanging, with holes drilled at intervals. Wooden beads were stitched through the hanging and the holes. The rest of the panel hangs loose.

This type of work lends itself to a variety of different mounting finishes.

PROJECT 12 WOOD KNOTS

Large panel in stitchery and machine quilting. Original 60 × 86cm. Worked in three separate sections, then joined together, making an impressive-looking panel, which is relatively easy to make. The original design was based on a large rubbing taken from a plank of wood and used actual size.

Requirements

Plasterer's scrim, 100 × 30cm (plus a generous turning)
Brown fabric to fit under scrim, 100 × 30cm (can be joined)
Brown fabric for central section, 100 × 30cm
Light golden-brown velvet for lower section, 100 × 30cm
Selection of threads—good variety of textures, wools, raffine, etc
Thick mounting board (lightweight), eg Sundela, 60 × 86cm
Bamboo rod or dowel, 90cm long
Thin backing fabric, 100 × 30cm
Interlining, 60 × 86cm
Copydex or UHU
Tailor's pencil

Method

1 Work the top section first, by mounting the scrim on a wooden frame for working (say an old picture frame). Fold the edges, then drawing-pin securely, as scrim frays easily.

2 Embroider the scrim freely with different-textured threads, using a simple darning and weaving stitch, and double thread. Pull a large hole, and secure with a few threads, to form the 'knot' in the wood. (Use a very long thread where possible to avoid joins, securing the thread at each side of the work.)

3 Remove scrim carefully from frame, and fix the second fabric section to the frame; mark in a few guidelines with a tailor's pencil, for stitching the flowing lines of the design. Embroider with a variety of threads and stitches—chain, twisted chain, stem, van-dyke (far left), with raised chain band for the 'knot'.

4 Work the lower section by tacking the velvet to the backing material, adding two extra lines across the width to hold it in place.

5 Mark a few guidelines for machining the lines of the design with tailor's pencil.

6 Starting in the centre, machine the marked lines.

7 Pad the 'knot' by slitting the backing and padding lightly with wadding. Close up the gap with a few over-casting stitches.

Making-up

8 Place the brown fabric under the scrim, and tack together.

9 Place the scrim and the middle section right sides together, and tack close to the embroidery. Machine together through the three layers of fabric.

10 Place the velvet section to the lower edge of the middle section, right sides together, and tack through the three fabrics. Machine close to the lines of the design.

11 Flatten the edges on the back of the work—but it is not necessary to trim them. Overcast to the backing fabric with sewing cotton.

12 Glue a piece of interfacing fabric to the top surface of the mounting board. Trim close to the edges.

13 Place the embroidery face-down on a clean surface, and put the interlined surface of the board to the wrong side of the embroidery.

14 Using Copydex or UHU, glue the edges of the fabric to the board, pulling the fabric taut. Continue as for basic mounting, finishing with hessian binding. Do not stitch top yet—leave open to insert tabs.

15 Make four tabs (see page 141) from matching fabric, eg velvet, and stitch them firmly at intervals. Check that enough space is left for the rod to pass through.

Detail of large 'Wood Knots' panel which was worked in three horizontal sections: top on coarse scrim, freely woven with threads; middle on woollen fabric with closed buttonhole stitch, cable chain and twisted chain, with central knot of raised chain band; and lower is machine-quilted velvet. By Audrey Babington (Ian Robson)

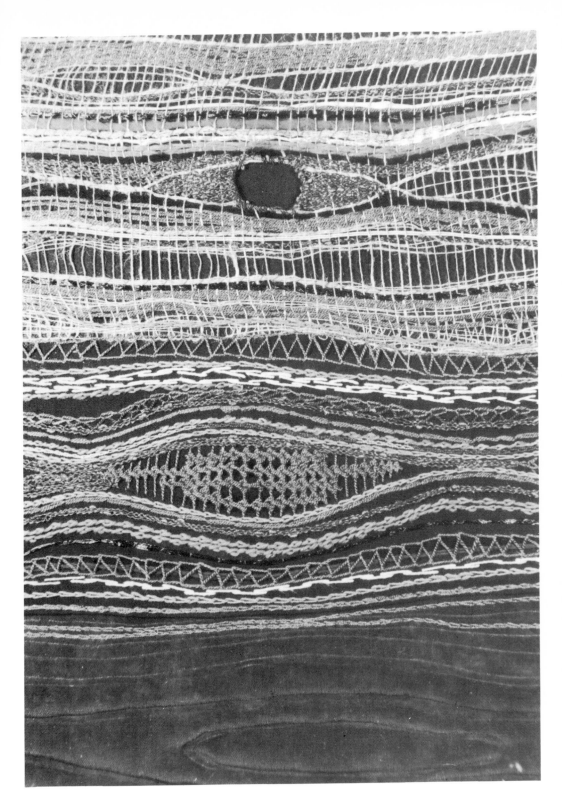

PROJECT 13 YOUNG RHINO

Stitchery and appliqué in a framed panel. Care is needed to fix the animal shape on card, and when applying it to background fabric.

Requirements

Pale grey woollen fabric for animal
Dark grey velvet for background
Selection of threads, a few wooden beads, small washers
Frame for working—old picture frame, artist's stretchers, etc
Inner window mount, veneered (optional)

Method

1 Cut a paper shape for the required size of the animal. Any shape could be used, provided the outer shape is simple, with no thin, long pieces. Draw lines on the body, dividing it into sections for stitchery.
2 Cut the same shape in stiff card.
3 Pin the paper shape on the grey fabric, which should have a good allowance all round for working.
4 Tack round the outlines of the shape and through the paper, on the lines marking the divisions on the body. Remove paper carefully.

'Young Rhino'. The veneered window mount of light oak picks up the colour of the wooden beads stitched on the animal's back; the outer frame echoes the colours of the threads used—grey, white and brown

5 Pin the fabric to the wooden frame with drawing-pins. Fill the sections with stitchery, placing beads and button-holed washers where required. The head is stitched with rows of chain stitch, altering the shades of grey, using three strands of embroidery cotton. The rest of the body is filled with a variety of threads and stitches, in greys, blues, tan and white.
6 Take out the tacking, and remove the work from the frame. Cut the shape out from the fabric, allowing 2–3cm turning.
7 Place the card shape on the embroidered animal (on wrong side, matching the shape carefully).
8 Using UHU or similar adhesive, secure the edges to the back of the card, making sure the work lies taut across the shape.
9 Fix the velvet fabric to a frame, making it taut. Pin the embroidered animal to the centre of the fabric, then stitch it to the fabric with a matching thread.
10 Stick the edges of the velvet to a hardboard base with adhesive, taking them to the back

166

of the hardboard. If you are using a veneered
window-mount, place this in position over
the velvet.

11 Place in the wooden frame, and neaten the
back by securing the board with brads, then
fixing a piece of card to cover the back of the
hardboard and brads, securing it with any
adhesive and then masking tape.

12 Fix screw eyes and hanging cord.

PROJECT 14 CIRCULAR WOOD KNOT

Woollen embroidery on scrim, using stem stitch
and couching. Original 21cm diameter. Design
taken from a wax-crayon rubbing (see page 45).

Requirements

Window-cleaner's scrim, 24cm diameter circle
Woollen threads, different thicknesses and textures
Wire lampshade ring, 21cm diameter
Large-eyed needles

Method

1 Pin the scrim over the wire lampshade ring,
turning under the edges and folding them right
round the wire. Catch-stitch down, using a
matching cotton (the stitches showing on the
right side will be hidden by the embroidery).

2 Mark in the main outlines of the stitching with
a fine felt pen or transfer pencil. Mark the
holes. See diagram overleaf.

3 Snip a small piece (the size of a small finger-
nail) from the large centre hole. Using a light-
coloured wool (single), overcast the hole, taking stitches $\frac{1}{2}$–1cm long, close together, taking
under the raw edges and enclosing them. Make
a few small slits in the scrim if the edges do not
turn under easily.

4 Make the smaller holes with a skewer, and
smaller stitches.

5 Embroider the wood knot with wools and
threads, using stem stitch and couching for
textured wools. If the wool is thin use it
double, and always work with a long thread,
starting at one edge of the ring, threading the
ends through the rolled hem, and finishing in
the same manner. This makes a very neat
finish on the back, with no ends showing.

6 When the stitching is completed, attach a
twisted wool thread at the back of the ring for
hanging. No other neatening or backing is
required.

Portion of 'Circular Wood Knot' design showing large off-centre hole, with smaller holes, the design's centre point and the main lines of stitching

168

PROJECT 15 MOSAIC

Suitable for a group project. This type of hanging can be made to any size and shape, depending on the number and size of the units. The original has 24 units, each 14cm square with slightly rounded corners, hung from a flat wooden rod 77cm long. The small individual units provide an opportunity to use up small quantities of fabrics, threads and beads, making a striking and interesting wall-hanging.

Requirements

24 pieces of thick card, 14cm square, with slightly rounded corners
24 pieces of thin backing card, 13·5cm square, with slightly rounded corners
A variety of plain fabrics, in a range of toning colours (used also for backing units)
Threads, wools, braids, cords, etc
Beads, buttons, washers, etc
24 large brass curtain rings (31mm)
5 small hanging hooks
Flat wooden rod, 77cm long (original stained dark brown)
UHU glue
Round wooden frame for working

Method

1 Tack the outline of the card shape to a piece of background fabric and fix it in the frame, pulling the fabric taut.
2 Build up a design, starting in the centre, using beads, thread-covered washers, etc. Couch the braids and other items around, and develop with stitchery, eg cretan, fly or herringbone. Each unit can have a different design, or the same one can be worked twice. By using an agreed selection of colours, with some unifying threads, the whole will blend together. (Note: a couched thread can be added when the work is partly mounted, to outline the shape of the card—see below.)
3 Cover one side of the *thick* pieces of card with a thin layer of wadding (or old blanket). Smear glue lightly round the edges of the card, then stick this interlining to it, cutting any surplus off level with the card.
4 Take the fabric out of the frame, and place it face-downwards on a clean surface. Cut out the shape of the card, allowing 3cm for turnings *beyond* the tacking lines. Place the cards lined side on the back of the design.

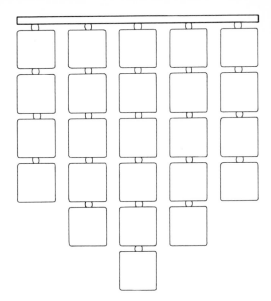

5 Snip fabric on rounded corners, then smear glue on the back of the card, round all four sides, and pull the edges of fabric over. Take out tacking threads.
6 Add any other decoration to the design, eg couched thread to outline the card shape. (A better shape is assured with the card in position.)
7 Make backing: cover a *thin* card shape with matching fabric by tacking this into place, stitching through the card.
8 Attach it to the back of the thick card by a small area of glue in the centre, then stitching the edges together—use double thread.
9 To complete the hanging, arrange the units in your preferred order. (The original had a centre line, hanging vertically, of six units, with five and four on either side.)
10 The units are attached to each other, and the rod, with curtain rings. Make a mark on each unit, top and bottom, in the centre, then snip the thread holding the two cards together, and push the ring in a short way. Stitch it to the edges, closing the gap securely.
11 The lower unit in each line could have a fringe, attached to a ring, added to the lower edge.
12 Position the five lines carefully together. Place the wooden rod in position, then mark the required position of the five hanging hooks on the back. Screw them into place, then hang each line of units on them.

169

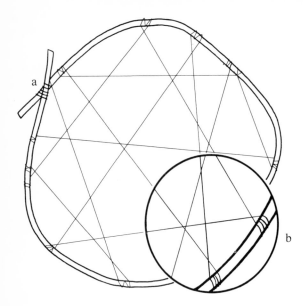

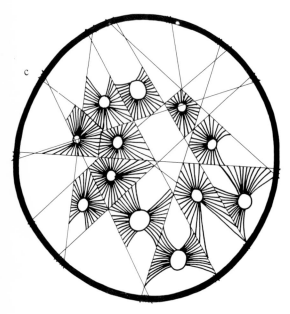

PROJECT 16 MACHINED OPENWORK

Individual or for a group mobile. Lacy openwork designs can be stitched by machine, without fabric, using a wire foundation which may be temporary or permanent. The design can be detached from the wire support, and then attached to a background fabric, or stitched to a rigid lampshade ring, as part of a group mobile. If a number are worked in different sizes and colours, they can be hung in various combinations, according to the space available. A temporary frame can be made with wire—millinery wire used double, or stiffer wire. Bind the ends securely (see point a in drawing)—the shape need not be precisely circular.

Requirements
Wire 'frame'
Sylko 40
Sewing machine prepared for free embroidery

Method
1 Thread the machine, top and bottom, with Sylko 40.
2 Draw up the bobbin thread and tie the two ends together, dipping the needle by moving the wheel by hand. Stitch four times over wire.
3 Stitch to the opposite side of the frame, and repeat the four stitches over the wire by hand, finishing on the opposite side to the direction the next line of stitching is to take (see point b on drawing). This keeps the stitches together, and stops them spreading.
4 Continue as above, working each line at approximate right angles to the last.
5 When enough lines have been worked to form a web, a pattern can be worked over it—spirals, or radiating circles (point c). If the openwork is to be left on the wire frame, fasten off any ends invisibly, then hang it up, either alone or in a group.
6 If it is to be removed from the wire, and applied, lay it in position on the background fabric, and slide both together under the needle.
7 Hold the wire firmly in position and sew several small stitches over each angle, just inside the wire.
8 Cut the wire carefully in several places, and slide it out. Do not cut the loops of thread—stitch them down or conceal them with couched thread, etc.

170

PROJECT 17 SEED TIME

Machine-embroidered panel. See colour picture, page 118, Satin-stitch 'beads' give a delicate effect which is only suitable for a panel, as the stretching of the fabric is essential for the tension of the linking thread. The speed should be constant and fairly fast—if the machine is run too slowly or irregularly, the thread or needle may break.

Requirements

Background fabric
Sylko 50—red, white and black
Wooden ring frame
Hardboard to chosen size for mounting
Swing-needle sewing machine

Method

1 Practise making some satin-stitch beads on a spare piece of fabric. Place it in the frame, making it drum-taut. Thread the needle with the cotton (do not use a thick thread or it will jam). Set the stitch lever to the widest setting, and lower the feed dog.

2 Draw up the lower thread, and hold both top and bottom thread and the frame, so that they do not move; then do a three or four second burst of stitching, to build up a bead.

3 Make the last stitch from the left to the right, turning the wheel by hand. Make another stitch 2mm away from the first 'bead' and repeat the process, making a line pattern. Any arrangement can be made—remember that the last stitch of a bead must finish on the side that the next one is to be started. Sometimes it will be necessary to dip the needle into the fabric twice, by hand, to ensure that the needle is swinging the correct way.

4 To make the seed design, work red and black 'beads' and long linking lines at random. The long thread is made by taking the tension off the needle and thread—by raising the presser-foot bar and lowering it again, positioning the needle for the next 'bead'.

5 Work a radiating pattern of seed heads in white thread, overlapping the other stitching.

6 Take the work out of the frame, and complete it as for basic mounting.

PROJECT 18 WALL SAMPLER

Soft hanging. Original 60 × 90cm excluding fringe, in shades of fawn-brown. A large hanging made for a City & Guilds course. The method described for making it can be used for a smaller hanging, altering the scale of the design. Although this is an ambitious project, inexperienced embroiderers have made similar ones with minimal help. Once the main design has been marked, any variety of stitches can be worked.

Requirements

Background fabric, 70 × 109cm (fine brown wool in original)
Selection of small pieces of contrasting fabrics
Selection of threads, including wools
Beads, sequins, etc
Interlining—duck calico, blanket, etc
Lining material to match background fabric

Method

1 Plan the design, by cutting different-sized squares of paper (see diagram overleaf). No 1: 17cm with window cut-out, 9cm. No 2: 12cm. No 3: 16cm with inner square, 6cm. No 4: 18cm. *Top right*: No 5: 16cm. No 6: 25cm, with inner square, 15cm and small square, 7cm. No 7: 14cm, cut-out window, 8cm. Nos 8 and 9, 6cm.

2 Pin squares to fabric (working flat on a table), grouping them so that the top and lower edges are aligned, and leaving sufficient space round them for extra lines of stitches. When completed, there should be a margin of clear fabric 4cm at the sides and 6cm at top and bottom.

3 Tack round outlines of squares. Remove papers (use them as templates).

4 *No 1:* work an inner rectangle of eyelets on a cream linen separately (use a round frame). Tack into position. Cut rectangle of dark fawn fabric (use iron-on Vilene if it frays). Tack over eyelets, then work in chainstitch on the inner edges, and blanket stitch on the outer edges, using a brown thread.

No 2: a 3cm square of brown felt is slipstitched in the centre, and surrounded with a log cabin arrangement of stitches—vandyke, cretan, closed feather, etc (see Patchwork page 80).

No 3: Norwich stitch is worked separately on a small piece of canvas, with thin, pale fawn wool (see page 71). Tuck in the edges of the canvas, tack into position, then secure with closed feather stitch. Work an outer row of closed feather stitch in pale fawn thread, then fill in the space with tiny glass beads.

No 4: laid work (see page 93 for stitches). Place this section of the background fabric in a frame, and work long stitches in dull yellow wool horizontally and vertically. Tie down with a small stitch where they cross. Add cross-stitches and beads in the spaces. Maltese tufts (page 99) add interest at the sides, worked in ginger wool.

No 5: mount this section of the background fabric in a frame, and work cloud stitch in a pale thread. White 'bubbly' wool is threaded up and down the rows to give added texture. A few large amber-coloured beads are added at random.

No 6: this square is the focal point of the design. A small square of velvet, mounted over a piece of card, is slipstitched in the centre. An outer frame of fawn needlecord (four straight strips) is hemmed into position, and the space between is filled with needleweaving, wooden beads and small shiny brown beads. Crested chain stitch and herringbone are worked round the edge of the needlecord frame. Couched thread and bugle beads extend this square still further.

No 7: an inner square of scrim, pulled into a pattern with four-sided stitch, is worked separately, in a frame. When worked, place a bright orange fabric underneath the scrim, then tack both into position. A light brown velvet frame is tacked into position, enclosing a small amount of padding. Chain stitch is worked over the raw edge, then knotted cable chain stitch.

Nos 8 and 9: blocks of Pekinese stitch and interlacing stitch, with Maltese tufts round them. Woven wheels are worked between 5 and 6, and 6 and 7.

Making up

5 Make up the hanging, as described in soft hangings, with interlining. Use a concealed wooden strip at the top and bottom of the work to give rigidity and extra weight.

6 The top is finished with a series of button-holed woollen loops, fitted with a stained dowel rod.

7 The lower edge is finished with a thick woollen fringe 14cm long (see section on fringes).

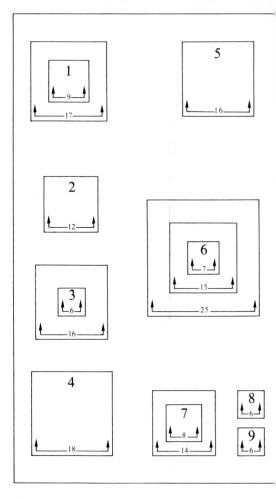

The squares to cut out

Brown Wall Sampler. By Audrey Babington (Ian Robson)

172

11 Care and Preservation Measures

Hangings are made for a variety of reasons and purposes—some are made quickly, others take months or years of time and effort. We have no way of knowing which will survive for future generations, so we can only try to provide some measure of care and protection. The Textile Conservation Centre advises:

1 Keep hangings away from direct sunlight and fluorescent-tube lighting.

2 Hangings, if lined, should be hanging without strain.

3 Excessive dryness, heat or damp, and moths, can cause fibres to weaken and rot.

4 Although there are various fabric preservers available, they are not recommended, as they may be harmful over a long period.

5 Cleaning of hangings can be done with a piece of nylon filament screening (approximately a metre square—it is fairly rigid, but frays easily, so bind the edges). Hold it above the hanging, and vacuum carefully, using the suction nozzle. Alternatively, fine net can be placed over the nozzle, but caution is required—do not hold the nozzle too near the hanging, or threads may be sucked up.

6 If the panel is glazed, the glass should be sealed in the frame; the textile should not touch the glass; the panel should be carefully sealed at the back against entry of dust.

Acknowledgements

I should like to thank the following people and organisations for giving generous help willingly:
J & P Coats for allowing me to use their stitch drawings;
English Sewing Ltd for instructions, drawings and photographs of machine embroidery;
Devon Brass Rubbing Centre for illustrations;
Dylon International;
Creative Knitting Council;
Embroiderers' Guild;
members of the 62 Group;
Surrey Federation of Women's Institutes;
Longleat House Press Office;
Wippell Mowbray Ltd;
Dryad;
A. J. Arnold & Sons Ltd;
Berol Ltd;
Guy St John Scott (Binney and Smith Ltd);
Polycell Ltd;
  Special thanks to Richard Carpenter, for photographing my work so expertly, and to David & Charles, for giving valuable help and advice, which improved the original manuscript.

Index